ISBN: 978129003966

Published by:
HardPress Publishing
8345 NW 66TH ST #2561
MIAMI FL 33166-2626

Email: info@hardpress.net
Web: http://www.hardpress.net

POEMS

VIZ.

An ODE to Lord Bolingbroke.
The SPLENDID SHILLING.
BLEINHEIM. *A Poem.*
CYDER, *In Two Books.*

By Mr. JOHN PHILIPS.

EDINBURGH:

Printed by Campbell Denovan, at his Printing
Office, Turk's Closs, Lawn-Market;
For Patrick Anderson, Bookseller,
Parliament-Square.
1778.

THE

L I F E

OF

MR. J O H N   P H I L I P S.

AFTER we have read the works of a poet with pleasure, and reflected upon them with improvement, we are naturally apt to inquire into his life, the manner of his education, and other little circumstances, which give a new beauty to his writings, and let us into the genius and character of their author. To satisfy this general inclination, and do some justice to the memory of Mr. PHILIPS, we shall give the world a short account of him and his few, but excellent, compositions. Sufficient they were, though few, to his fame, but not to our wishes.

A 2

He was the fon of Dr STEPHEN PHILIPS, arch-deacon of Salop, and born at Bampton in Oxford-fhire, December the thirtieth, Anno 1676. After he was well grounded in grammar-learning, he was fent to Winchefter fchool, where he made himfelf mafter of the Latin and Greek languages, and was foon diftinguifhed for a happy imitation of the excellencies which he difcovered in the beft claffical authors.

With this foundation of good learning, and very early promifes of a farther improvement in all ufe-ful ftudies, he was removed to Chrift-Church in Oxford. From his firft entrance into that univer-fity, he was very much efteemed for the fimplicity of his manners, the agreeablenefs of his converfa-tion, and the uncommon delicacy of his genius. All his univerfity exercifes were received with ap-plaufe; and in that place, fo famous for good fenfe, and a true fpirit, he, in a fhort time, grew to be fu-perior to moft of his cotemporaries: where, to have been their equal only, had been a fufficient praife. There it was, that, following the natural bent of his genius, befide other valuable authors, he became acquainted with Milton, whom he ftudied with ap-plication, and traced him in all his fuccefsful tran-flations from the antients. There was not an al-lufion in his PARADISE LOST, drawn from the thoughts or expreffions of Homer or Virgil, which he could not immediately refer to; and, by that, he perceived what a peculiar life and grace, their fentiments added to English poetry; how much their images raifed its fpirit; and what weight and beauty their words, when tranflated, gave to its language. Nor was he lefs curious in obferving the force and elegancy of his mother-tongue, but, by the example of his darling Milton, fearched backwards into the works of our old Englifh poets, to furnifh himfelf with proper founding, and fignificant expreffions, and prove the due extent, and compafs of the language. For this purpofe, he carefully read over Chaucer, and Spenfer; and, afterwards, in his writings, did not fcruple to revive any words, or phrafes, which he thought deferved it, with that modeft liberty, which Horace allows of, either in the coining of new, or reftoring of ancient expreffions. Yet though he was a profeffed admirer of thefe authors, it was not from any view of appearing in public; for fuch was his modefty, that he was the only perfon who did not think himfelf qualified for it: he read for his own pleafure; and writing was the only thing he declined, wherein he was capable of pleafing others. Nor was he fo in love with poetry, as to neglect any other parts of good literature, which either their ufefulnefs, or his own genius, excited him to purfue. He was very well verfed in the whole compafs of natural philofophy; and feemed, in his ftudies, as well as his writings, to have made Virgil his pattern, and often to have broke out with him into the following rapturous wifh;

Me vero primum dulces ante omnia Mufae,
Quarum facra fero ingenti perculfes amore,
Accipiant; coelique vias et fidera monftrent;
Défeĉtus folis varios, lunaeque labores:
Undè tremor terris; qua vi maria alta tumefcant
Objicibus ruptis, rurfufque in fe ipfa refidant:
Quid tantum oceano properent fe tingere foles
Hyberni; vel quae tardis mqra noĉtibus obftet.

Georg. lib. II.

Give me the ways of wand'ring ftars to know,
The depths of heaven above, and earth below,
Teach me the various labours of the moon,
And whence proceed th' eclipfes of the fun.
Why flowing tides prevail upon the main,
And in what dark recefs they fhrink again.
What fhakes the folid earth, what caufe delays
The fummer nights, and fhortens winter days.

DRYDEN.

Mr Philips was no lefs paffionate an admirer of nature; and it is probable, that he drew his own character, in that defcription which he gives of a philofophical and retired life, at the latter end of the firft book of his * CYDER.

——He to his labours hies, .
Gladfome, intent on fomewhat that may eafe
Unhealthy mortals, and with curious fearch
Examines all the properties of herbs,
Foffils, and minerals, that th' embowell'd earth
Difplays, if by his induftry he can
Benefit human race.——

And we have good reafon to believe, that much might have been attained to, many new difcoveries made, by fo diligent an enquirer, and fo faithful a recorder of phyfical operations. However, though death prevented our hopes in that refpect, yet the admirable paffages of that kind, which we find in his poem on CYDER, may convince us of the nicenefs of his obfervations in natural caufes: befide this, he was particularly fkilled in all manner of antiquites, efpecially thofe of his own country; and part of this too,

* Firft printed Anno 1708.

he has, with much art and beauty, intermixed
with his poetry.

As to his private character, he was beloved by
all that knew him, and admired by thofe who did
not; fomewhat referved, and filent among ftran-
gers, but free, familiar, and eafy with his friends:
the firft was, the effect of his modefty; the latter, of his chearful innocence: the one was, the
proper caution of a wife man; the other, the
good-humour of a friend. He was averfe to con-
tentious difputes; and thought no time fo ill
fpent, and no wit fo ill ufed, as that which was
employed in fuch debates. Thus he never con-
tributed to the uneafinefs of his company, but
often to their inftruction, always to their pleafure. As on the one hand, he declined all ftrokes
of fatire; fo, on the other, he detefted flattery
as much; and, I believe, would rather have
been contented with the character of a dull man,
than that of a witty, or fervile one, at the ex-
pence of his humanity, or fincerity. This fincerity, indeed, was his diftinguifhing character;
and made him as dear to all good men, as his
wit and learning did to all favourers of true fenfe,
and letters.

Upon all thefe accounts, during his ftay in the
univerfity, he was honoured with the acquaint-

ance of the beft and politeft men in it ; many of
whom, who now make confiderable figures, both
in the ftate, and in the republic of learning, would
think it no difgrace to have their names mentioned, as Mr. Philips' friends. And here we muft
not omit that particular friendfhip which he con-
tracted with Mr. Edmund Smith, author of the
incomparable tragedy of PHAEDRA and HIPPO-
LITUS; and who, upon his deceafe, celebrated
his memory in a fine poem ; and foon after followed him to the grave. Thefe two often com-
municated their thoughts to each other ; and as
their ftudies lay the fame way, were much to
their mutual fatisfaction, and improvement. For,
as the mind takes no greater pleafure than in a
free and unreferved difcovery of its own notions,
fo it can reap no greater profit than in the cor-
rection it meets with from the judgement of a fincere friend. This, we make no doubt, was as
pleafant as any part of Mr. Philips' life, who had
a foul capable of relifhing all the fineft enjoyments
of fublime, virtuous, and elegant fpirits. I am
fure Mr. Smith, in his poem to his memory,
fpeaks of it as what moft affected him, and pa-
thetically complains for the lofs of it.

Whom ſhall I find unbyaſs'd in diſpute,
Eager to learn, unwilling to confute ?
To whom the labours of my ſoul diſcloſe,
Reveal my pleaſure, or diſcharge my woes ?
O ! in that heav'nly youth for ever ends
The beſt of ſons, of brothers, and of friends.

It is to be deplored, indeed, that two great ge-
niuſes, in whoſe power it was to have obliged the
world ſo much, ſhould make ſo ſhort a ſtay in it ;
though had their date been longer, we can hardly ſay, that time would have added any thing but
number to their compoſitions. It was their happi-
neſs to give us all their pieces perfect in their kind;
the accuracy of their judgement not ſuffering them
to publiſh without the greateſt care and correct-
neſs. For haſty fruits, the common product of
every injudicious fancy, ſeldom continue long, never come to maturity, and are, at beſt, food only
for debauched and vitiated palates. Theſe men
thought, and conſidered before they ſat down to
write; and after they had written too, being ever
the laſt perſons who were ſatisfied that they had
performed well: and even then, perhaps, more in
compliment to the opinion of others, than from
the conviction of their own judgements.

But it is now time that we lead our author from
his univerſity friend to ſome of a higher rank, among

whom he met with an equal applaufe and admiration. The reafon of his coming to town, was the perfuafion of fome great perfons, who engaged him to write upon the battle of Bleinheim*; and, how well their expectations were anfwered, it will be more proper to mention when we fpeak of his works.   It is enough at prefent to obferve, that this poem brought him into favour and efteem with † two of the moft eminent encouragers and patrons of letters that have appeared in our age : the one, famous for his political knowledge and univerfal learning; the other, diftinguifhed for the different talents of a refined and polite genius, and an indefatigable application to bufinefs, joined with an exquifite and fuccefsful penetration in affairs of the higheft concern.

However, though he was much refpected by thefe, and other noble patrons, yet from the modeft diftruft he entertained of himfelf, it was not without fome pain that he enjoyed their company, and the fear of offending oftentimes made him lefs ftudious of pleafing.   Such was the humble opinion he conceived of his own good qualities, that it made them lefs confpicuous to others ; as if he was afhamed that his virtues were greater ;

---

* Anno 1705.
† The late earl of Oxford, and lord Bolingbroke.

he chofe rather to obfcure thofe which he really
had, than to place them in that ornamental light
which they deferved. I fpeak this only with refpect to his converfation with his fuperiors, who,
knowing his true worth, were more pleafed with
his endeavours to difguife it, than if he had fet it
off with all the oftentatious gaiety that men of much
wit, but little humility and good-breeding, generally affect. As this decent filence did not prejudice the great againft his wit, fo neither did his
unfolicitous eafinefs in his fortune at all hinder the
marks of their favour and munificence. True it
is, that he never praifed any one with a fordid
view, nor ever facrificed his fincerity to his intereft,
having a foul above ennobling the vicious ; and
as he gave his characters with the fpirit of a poet,
he obferved at the fame time the fidelity of an
hiftorian. This, indeed, was a part which diftinguifhed him as much from almoft all other poets,
as his manner of writing did ; he being one of
thofe few who were equally averfe to flattery and
detraction. He never went out of his way for a
panegyric, or forced his invention to be fubfervient to his gratitude; but interwove his characters
fo well with the thread of his poetry, and adapted
them fo juftly to the merit of the perfons, that
they all appear natural, beautiful, and of a piece

with the poem. If it be reckoned difficult to praife well, for our author not to err, in fuch a variety, is much more fo, and looks like the mafterly hand of a great painter, who can draw all forts of beauties, and at the fame time that he gives them their proper charms, happily diftinguifhes them from each other. In fhort, to purfue the metaphor, there is nothing gaudy in his colours, nothing ftiff or affected in his manner; and all the lineaments are fo exact, that an indifferent eye may, at firft view, difcover who fat for the picture.

From this general view of his writings, I fhall now pafs on to a particular; of which it is to be wifhed, there were a larger, as well as a better, than the following account. I have heard a ftory of an eminent preacher, who, out of an obftinate modefty, could never be prevailed upon to print but one fermon *, (the beft, perhaps, that ever paffed the prefs) to which the public gave the title of Dr. CRADOCK's WORKS. The fame, with much juftice, might be given to the poetical compofitions which our excellent author has publifh- ed, and which may challenge that name more

B

* On Providence. Preached before K. Charles II. Feb. 10. 1677-8.

defervedly, than all the mighty volumes of profufe and negligent writers.

The firft of thefe was the SPLENDID SHIL-
LING; a title as new and uncommon for a poem,
as his way of adorning it was, and which, in the
opinion of one of the beft and moft unprejudicial
judges of this age, " is the fineft burlefque poem
" in the Britifh language*." Nor was it only
the fineft of that kind in our tongue, but handled
in a manner quite different from what had been
made ufe of by any author of our own, or other
nations; the fentiments and ftile being in this
both new; whereas in thofe, the jeft lies more
in allufions to the thoughts and fables of the an-
cients, than in the pomp of the expreffion. The
fame humour is continued through the whole,
and not unnaturally diverfified, as moft poems of
that nature have been before. Out of that variety
of circumftances, which his fruitful invention
muft fuggeft to him on fuch a fubject, he has not
chofen any but what are diverting to every reader,
and fome, that none but his inimitable drefs
could have made diverting to any. When we
read it, we are betrayed into a pleafure that we
could not expect; though at the fame time, the
fublimity of the ftile, and gravity of the phrafe,

* See the Tatler, Numb. 250.

feem to chaftife that laughter which they provoke.

In her beft light the comic mufe appears,
When fhe, with borrow'd pride, the bufkin wears*.

This was the firft piece that made him known
to the world; and, though printed from an incor-
rect copy, gained him an univerfal applaufe; and
(as every thing new in its kind does) fet many
imitators to work ; yet none ever came up to the
humour and happy turn of the original. A genuine edition of it came out fome years after; for
he was not fo folicitous for praife, as to haften even
that, which by the earneft he received from the
public, he might modeftly affure himfelf would
be a procurer of it.

The next of his poems was that, intitled
BLEINHEIM ; wherein he fhews, that he could
ufe the fame fublime and nervous ftile as proper-
ly on a ferious and heroic fubject, as he had before done on one of a more light and ludicrous
nature. We have faid before, at whofe requeft
this was wrote ; though he would willingly have
declined that undertaking, had not the powerful
incitements of his friends prevailed upon him, to

B 2

* See Mr. Smith's Poem above mentioned.

give up his modefty to their judgement.   The ex-
ordium of this piece is a juft allufion to the beginning of the Æneid, (if that be Virgil's) and
that of Spencer's FAIRY QUEEN.

From low and abject themes, the grove'ling mufe
Now mounts aerial, to fing of arms
Triumphant, and emblaze the martial acts
Of Britain's hero ; —

The fpirit is kept on the fame to the end ; the
whole being full of noble fentiments, and majeftic
numbers, equal to the Hero whom it extols ; and
not admitting of any rival, (except Mr. Addifon's
poem*) on the fame occafion.   I cannot forbear
mentioning one beautiful imitation of Virgil in
his digreffion upon the poetical Elizium, where
the famous——Tu Marcellus eris——is fo happily tranflated and applied, that it fhews the fpirit
of Virgil better than all the labours of his com-
mentators : there, fpeaking of the late marquifs
of Blandford, he fays ;

Had thy prefiding ftar propitious fhone,
Shouldft CHURCHILL be !——

The addreffes to his patrons are very fine and
artificial: the firft, juft and proper; and the latter

* The Campaign.

of Englifh Memmius, exactly appofite to him, to-whom all the polite part of mankind agree, in applying that of the Roman ;

———Quem tu dea tempore in omni
Omnibus ornatum voluifti excellere rebus.

As to his CYDER, it is one (if not the only) fi-nifhed poem, of that length, extant in our lan-guage ; the foundation of that work was laid, and the firft book compofed at Oxford; the fecond, was for the moft part, in town. He determined to the choice of that fubject, by the violent paffion he had to do fome honour to his native country ; and has therefore exerted all the powers of genius and art to make it complete. It is founded upon the mo-del of VIRGIL's GEORGICS; and comes the near-eft of any other, to that admirable poem, which the critics prefer to the divine Æneid. Yet, though it is eafy to difcern who was his guide in that dif-ficult way, we may obferve, that he comes after rather like a purfuer, than a follower, not tracing him ftep after ftep, but chofing thofe paths in which he might eafieft overtake him. All his imi-tations are far from being fervile, though fome-times very clofe ; at other times, he brings in a new variety, and entertains us with fcenes more

B 3

unexpected and pleasing, perhaps, than his ma-
sters themselves were to those who first saw that
work. The conduct and management are superior
to all other copyers of that original; and, even
the admired Rapin is much below him, both in
design and success; for the Frenchman either fills
his gardens with the idle fables of antiquity, or
new transformations of his own; and has, in con-
tradiction to his own rules of criticism, judici-
ously blended the serious and sublime style of Virgil, with the elegant turns of Ovid in his Meta-
morphoses. Nor has the great genius of Mr.
Cowley succeeded better in his books of Plants,
who, besides the same faults with the former, is
continually varying his numbers from one sort of
verse to another, and alluding to remote hints of
medicinal writers, which, though allowed to be
useful, are yet so numerous, that they flatten the
dignity of the verse, and sink it from a poem to
a treatise of physic. It is not out of envy to the
merit of these great men (and who will ever be
such in spite of envy) that we take notice of these
mistakes, but only to shew the judgement of him
who followed them, in avoiding to commit the
same. Whatever scenes he presents us with,
appear delicate and charming; the philosophi-
cal touches surprize, the moral instruct, and the

gay defcriptions tranfport the reader. Sometimes
he opens the bowels of the earth ; at others, he
paints its furface ; fometimes he dwells upon its
lower products, and fruits ; at others, mounts to
its higher and more ftately plantations, and then
beautifies it with the innocent pleafures of its inhabitants. Here we are taught the nature and variety of foils ; there the difference of vegetables,
the fports of a rural, the retirement of a contemp-
lative life, the working genius of the hufbandman,
the induftry of the mechanic, contribute as much
to diverfify, as the due praifes of exalted patriots,
heroes, and ftatefmen, to raife and ennoble the
poetry. The change of feafons, and their diftinc-
tions, introduced by the rifing and fetting of the
ftars, the effects of heat, cold, fhowers, and tempefts, are in their feveral places very ornamental,
and their defcriptions inferior only to thofe of
Virgil.

It would be difficult, as well as ufelefs, to give
particular inftances of his imitations of the laft
mentioned poet : men of tafte and learning will
themfelves obferve them with pleafure ; and it
would be to no purpofe to quote them to the il-
literate : to the one, it would be a fort of an af-
front ; to the other, but an infipid entertainment.
Milton, we are informed, could repeat the beft

part of Homer; and the perfon of whom we write,. could do the fame of Virgil, and by continually reading him, fortunately equalled the variety of his numbers. This alone ought to be a fufficient anfwer to thofe who wifh this poem had been wrote in rhime, fince then it muft have loft half its beauties; it being impoffible, but that the fame undiftinguifhable tenour of verfification, and returns of clofe, fhould make it very unharmonious to a judicious and mufical ear. The beft judges of our nation have given their opinions againft rhime, even they, who ufed it with the greateft admiration and fuccefs, could not forbear condemning the practice. I am not ignorant, to what a height fome modern writers have carried this art, and adapted it to exprefs the moft fublime ideas; yet this has been in much fhorter poems than the prefent; and I doubt not but the fame perfons would have rejected it, were they to write upon the like occafion. I fhall not fo far enter into the difpute concerning the preference of thefe different manners of writing, as to ftate and anfwer the objections on each fide. It is true, Mr. Dryden thought that Milton's choice of blank verfe proceeded from his inability to rhime well; and, as good a reafon might eafily be given for his own choice; it being certain, he had the

perfect art and myftery of one, and could have
been but fecond in the other.

However, we leave this queftion to be decided
by thofe, whofe ftudies and defigns to excel in
poetry may oblige them to a more exact enquiry :
For my part, I think it no more a difreputation
to Mr. Philips, that he did not write in rhime,
than it is to Virgil, that he has not compofed
odes or elegies. The bent of out genius is what
we ought to purfue ; and if we anfwer our defigns
in that, it is fufficient. The critics would make
a man laugh, to hear him gravely difputing from
little hints of thofe authors, whether Virgil could
not have wrote better fatires, or Horace a good
epic poem.

But to return from this digreffion to my defign,
I would not have it thought that I prefume to make
a criticifm upon the works of our author, or thofe
of others. Thefe are only the fentiments of one
who is indifferent how they are received, if they
have the good fortune not to prejudice his memory,
for whofe fake they were written. I fhall add but
one remark more upon this fubject, which is the
great difficulty of making our Englifh names of
plants, foils, animals, and inftruments, fhine in
verfe : there are hardly any of thofe, which, in

the Latin tongue, are not in themfelves beautiful
and expreffive; and very few in our own, which
do not rather debafe than exalt the ftile. And yet,
I know not by what art of the poet, thefe words,
though in themfelves mean and low, feem not to
fink the dignity of his ftile, but became their
places as well as thofe of a better and more har-
monious found.

I cannot leave the CYDER, without taking notice, that the two books are addreffed to two gen-
tlemen, of whom it is enough to fay, that they
were Mr. Philips' friends and favourers, and
whofe characters, without the help of a weaker
hand, will be tranfmitted to pofterity. Nor muft
we omit that fignal honour which this piece received after his deceafe, in being tranflated into
Italian by a nobleman of Florence, an honour
which the great Boileau was proud his art of
poetry obtained, in a language of much lefs delicacy and politenefs*. It may be fome pleafure
to obferve the turn which Mr. Smith gives this
paffage in the following verfes † :

* Monfieur Boileau's ART OF POETRY was tranflated
into Portuguefe by the count de Ericeyra.

† See Mr. Smith's Poem on his death.

See mighty Cofmo's counfellor and friend,
By turns on Cofmo, and the bard attend:
Rich in the coins and bufts of antient Rome,
In him he brings a nobler treafure home ;
In them he views her gods, and domes defign'd, ⸮
In him the foul of Rome, and Virgil's mighty
To him for eafe retires from toils of ftate, (mind:
Not half fo proud to govern as tranflate. ⸌

All that we have left more of this poet is a
Latin ODE, infcribed to the honourable Henry
Saint John, Efq; late lord Bolingbroke, which is
certainly a mafter-piece: the ftile is pure and elegant, the fubject of a mixed nature, refembling
the fublime fpirit, and gay facetious humour of
Horace. From this we may form a judgement,
that his writings in that language were not inferior to thofe he has left us in our own ; and as
Horace was one of his darling authors, we need
not queftion his ability to excel in his way, as well
as that of the admired Virgil.

By all the enquiry I could make, I have not
found that he ever wrote any thing more than
what we have mentioned, nor indeed if there are
any, am I very folicitous about them, being con-
vinced that thefe are all which he finifhed, and
it would be an injury to his afhes to print any

imperfect sketches which he never designed for the public. It might, perhaps, please some to see the first essays of a great genius, but considering how apt we are to impose upon ourselves and others in matters of that kind, it is unfair to hazard the reputation of the writer for the fancy of the reader. It is a silly vanity that some men have delighted in, of informing the world how young they were when they composed some particular pieces; if they were not good, it is no matter at what age they were wrote; and if they are, it is a great chance, if they proceed, if they do not write beneath themselves.

We have almost as little to say in respect of our author's farther designs, only that we are assured by his friends, that he intended to write a Poem upon the Resurrection, and the Day of Judgement, in which it is probable, he would not only have exceeded all other, but even his own performances. That subject, indeed, was only proper to be treated of in that solemn stile which he makes use of, and by one whose just notions of religion, and true spirit of poetry, could have carried his reader, without a wild enthusiasm,

—Extra flammantia mænia mundi.   Lucret.

Milton has given a few fine touches upon the fame; but ftill there remains an inexhauftible, ftore of materials to be drawn from the prophets, the pfalmifts, and the other infpired writers, which, in his poetical drefs, might, without the falfe boafting of old poets, have endured to the DAY that it defcribed. The meaneft foul, and the loweft imagination, cannot think of that time, and the defcriptions we meet with of it in holy writ, without the greateft emotion, and the deepeft impreffion. What then might we not expect from the believing heart of a good man, and the regulated flights and raptures of an excellent Chriftian poet? His friend, Mr Smith, feems to be of the fame opinion; and as he was a better judge of the fcheme which he had laid down, and probably had feen the firft rudiments of his defign, we fhall finifh this head with his verfes on that occafion:

O! had relenting heaven prolong'd his days,
The tow'ring bard had fung in nobler lays,
How the laft trumpet wakes the lazy dead,
How faints aloft the crofs triumphant fpread;
How op'ning heavens their happy regions fhow,
And yawning gulphs with flaming vengeance glow,
And faints rejoice above, and finners howl below.

C

Well might he fing the DAY he could not fear,
And paint the glories he was fure to wear.

Thofe who have had either any knowledge of
his perfon, or relifh of his compofitions, will eafily agree in the judgement here given, as the ge-
nerality of men of fenfe and learning have already done in refpect of thofe which he lived to pu-
blifh. For my part, I never heard but of one * who
took it in his head to cenfure his writings ; and
it is no great compliment to his judgement, that
he has the honour to ftand alone in that reflec-
tion. It were eafy to retort upon him, were it
not ungenerous to blaft the fruits of his latter
fpring, † by comparing them with the crudities
of the firft. That fatire upon our author has,
with its other brethren, been dead long fince ;
and, I believe, the world would have quite forgot that ever it had had any being, had not Mr.
Smith taken care to inform us of it in a ‡ work
of a more durable nature.

* Sir Richard Blackmore.
† CREATION. A Poem.
‡ His poem to the memory of Mr. PHILIPS.

N. B. There was alfo a very filly anonymous piece wrote
    againft Mr. Philips' CYDER, called MILTON's SUBLIMITY
    ASSERTED, &c. but it died in the birth, or might be
    rather faid to be ftill-born, 1709.

However, though there is this one unjuft exception to his writings, there is none to his life, which was diftinguifhed by a natural goodnefs, a well-grounded and unaffected piety, an univerfal charity, and a fteady adherence to his principles. No one obferved the natural and civil duties of life with a ftricter regard, whether thofe of a fon, a friend, or a member of a fociety; and he had the happinefs to fill every one of thefe parts without even the fufpicion either of undutifulnefs, infincerity, or difrefpect. Thus he continued to the laft, not owing his virtues to the happinefs of his conftitution, but the frame of his mind; infomuch, that during a long and lingering ficknefs, which is apt to ruffle the fmootheft temper, he never betrayed any difcontent or uneafinefs, the integrity of his heart ftill preferved the cheerfulnefs of his fpirits. And if his friends had meafured their hopes of his life only by his unconcernednefs in his ficknefs, they could not but conclude, that either his date would be much longer, or that he was at all times prepared for death.

He had long been troubled with a lingering confumption, attended with an afthma; and the fummer before he died, by the advice of his phyficians, he went to the Bath, where, although he had the affiftance of the ableft of the faculty, by whom he was generally beloved, he only got fome prefent eafe; and returned from thence, but with fmall hopes of a recovery; and, upon the relapfe of his diftempers, he died at Hereford the 15th of February enfuing, Anno 1708.

He was interred in that cathedral; and the following infcription is upon his grave-ftone,

J O H A N N I S　P H I L I P S

Obiit 15 die Feb. Anno $\begin{cases} \text{Dom. 1708.} \\ \text{Ætat. fuae 32.} \end{cases}$

Cujus
Offas fi requiras, hanc urnam infpice,,
Si ingenium nefchias, ipfius opera confule,
Si tumulum defideras, templum adi Weftmonafterienfe·
Qualis quantufque vir fuerit,
Dicat elegans illa et præclara;
Quae conotaphium ibi decorat
Infcriptio.
Quam interim erga cognatos pius et officiofus,
Teftetur hoc faxum
A Maria Philips matre ipfius pientiffima,
Dilecti filii memoriæ non fine lacrymis dicatum.

The monument referred to at Weftminfter, in the foregoing infcription, ftands between thofe of Chaucer and Drayton, and was erected to his memory by Sir Simon Harcourt, late lord chancellor; an honour fo much the greater, as proceeding from one, who knew as well how to diftinguifh men, as excel them, and dealt out the marks of his refpect as impartially as he did the awards of his juftice. The epitaph was written by bifhop Atterbury, in a fpirit and ftile peculiar to his compofitions, viz.

Herefordiae conduntur offa,
  Hoc in delubro ftatuitur imago,
Britanniam omnem pervagatur fama
    JOHANNIS PHILIPS:
Qui viris bonis doctifque juxta charus,
  Immortale fuum ingenium,
  Eruditione multiplici excultum,
  Miro animi candore,
  Eximia morum fimplicitate,
    Honeftavit.
  Literarum amoeniorum fitim,
  Quam Wintoniae puer fentire coeperat,
Inter Aedis Chrifti alumnos jugiter explevit,
  In illo mufarum domicilio
  Preclaris aemulorum ftudiis excitatus,
Optimis fcribendi magiftris femper intentus,

Carmina fermone patrio compofuit ,
A Graecis Latinifque fontibus feliciter deducta,
  Atticis Romanifque auribus omnino digna,
    Verfuum quippe harmoniam ,
        Rythmo didicerat.
    Antiquo illo, libero, multiformi
  Ad res ipfas apto prorfus, et attemperato,
Non numeris in eundem fere orbem redeuntibus
Non claufularum fimiliter cadentium fono
            Metiri ;
Uni in hoc laudis genere, Miltono fecundus.
        Primoque poene par.
Res feu tenues, feu grandes, feu mediocres
      Ornandas fumpferat,
      Nufquam, non quod decuit,
      Et videt, et affecutus eft,
Egregius, quocunque ftylum verteret,
Fandi auctor, modorum artifex.
            Fas fit huic,
    Aufo licet a tua metrorum lege difcedere
O poefis Anglicanae pater, atque conditur Chaucere,
        Alterum tibi latus claudere,
Vatum certe cineres, tuos undique ftipantium
      Non dedicebit chorum.
SIMON HARCOURT miles, ·
  Viri bene de fe, deque literis meriti
      Quoad viveret, fautor,
      Poft obitum pie memor,
      Hoc illi faxum poni voluit.

J. Philis, Stephani, S. T. P. Archidiaconi
Salop, filius; natus est Bamptoniæ in agro
Oxon. Dec. 30. 1676.

Obiit Herefordiæ. Febr. 15. 1708.

Thus much we have thought proper to speak
of the life and character of Mr. Philips; following truth in every part, and endeavouring to
make both him, and his writings, an example to
others; or, if that cannot be attained through our
own defect, at least to shew, that a good poet
and a good man are not names always incon-
sistent.

GEO. SEWELL.

O D E

A D

HENRICUM St. JOHN, Armig.

I.

O Qui recifae finibus Indicis
  Benignus herbae, das mihi divitem
  Haurire fuccum, et fuaveolentes
  Saepe tubis iterare fumos;

II.

Qui folus acri refpicis afperum
Siti palatum, proluis et mero,
  Dulcem elaborant cui faporem
  Hefperii pretiumque, foles:

III.

Ecquid reponam muneris omnium
Exors bonorum ? Prome reconditum,
   Pimplaea, carmen, defidefque
   Ad numeros, age, tende, chordas.

IV.

Ferri fecundo mens avet impetu,
Qua cygniformes per liquidum aethera,
   Te, diva, vim praebente, vates
   Explicuit Venufinus alas :

V.

Solers modorum, feu puerum, trucem,
Cum matre flava, feu caneret rofas
   Et vina, Cyrrhaeis Hetrufcum
   Rite beans equitem fub antris.

VI.

At non Lyaei vis generofior
Affluxit illi ; faepe licet cadum
   Jactet Falernum, faepe Chiae
   Munera, laetitiamque teftae.

VII.

Patronus illi non fuit artium
Celebriorum ; fed nec amantior,

Nec charus aeque, O ! quae medullas
Flamma fubit, tacitofque fenfus,

VIII.

Pertentat, ut teque et tua munera
Gratus recordor, Mercurialium
   Princeps virorum ! et ipfae
   Cultor, et ufque colende mufis !

IX.

Sed me minantem grandia deficit
Receptus aegre fpiritus, ilia
   Dum pulfat ima, ac inquietum
   Tuffis agens fine more pectus.

X.

Alte petito quaffat anhelitu ;
Funefta plane, ni mihi balfamum
   Diftillet in venas, tuaeque
   Lenis opem ferat hauftus uvae.

XI.

Hanc fumo, parcis et tibi poculis
Libo falutem, quin precor, optima
   Ut ufque conjux fofpitetur,
   Perpetuo recreans amore,

XII.

Te confulentem militiae fuper
Rebus togatum.   Macte! Tori decus
   Formofa cui Francifca ceffit,
   Crine placens, niveoque collo!

XIII.

Quam gratiarum cura decentium
O! O! labellis cui Venus infidet!
   Tu forte felix ; me Maria
   Macerat (ah miferum !) videndo

XIV.

Maria, quae me fidereo tuens
Obliqua vultu per medium jecur
   Trajecit, atque excuffit omnes
   Protinus ex animo puellas.

XV.

Hanc, ulla mentis fpe mihi mutuae
Utcunque defit, nocte, die vigil
   Sufpiro ; nec jam vina fomnos
   Nec revocant, tua dona, fumi.

A N

O D E

T O

HENRY St. JOHN, Efq.

Tranflated by THOMAS NEWCOMB, A. M.

I.

O Thou from India's fruitful foil,
That doft that fovereign herb * prepare,
In whofe rich fumes I lofe the toil
Of life, and every anxious care :
While from the fragrant lighted bole,
I fuck new life into my foul.

D

* TOBACCO.

II.

Thou, only thou ! art kind to view
　　The parching flames that I fuftain ;
Which with cool draughts thy cafks fubdue
　　And wafh away the thirfty pain,　　• (prize,
　　　With wines, whofe ftrength and tafte we
　　　From Latian funs and nearer fkies.

III.

O ! fay, to blefs thy pious love,
　　What vows, what off'rings fhall I bring ?
Since I can fpare, and thou approve
　　No other gift, O hear me fing !
　　　In numbers Phœbus does infpire,
　　　That ftrings for thee the charming lyre.

IV.

Aloft, above the liquid fky,
　　I ftretch my wing, and fain would go
Where Rome's fweet fwan did whilom fly ;
　　And foaring, left the clouds below ;
　　　The mufe invoking to indue
　　　With ftrength, his pinions, as he flew.

V.

Whether he fings great beauty's praife,
 Love's gentle pain, or tender woes ;
Or chufe, the fubject of his lays,
 The blufhing grape, or blooming rofe ;
  Or near cool Cyrrha's rocky fprings,
  Mæcenas liftens while he fings.

VI.

Yet he no nobler draught could boaft,
 His mufe, or mufic to infpire,
Though all Falernum's purple coaft
 Flow'd in each glafs, to lend him fire :
  And on his tables us'd to fmile
  The vintage of each Chio's ifle.

VII.

Mæcenas deign'd to hear his fongs,
 His mufe extoll'd, his voice approv'd ;
To thee a fairer fame belongs,
 At once more pleafing, more belov'd.
  O ! teach my heart to bound its flame,
  As I record thy love and fame.

VIII.

Teach me the paffion to reftrain,
   As I my grateful homage bring :
And laft in Phœbus' humble train
   The firft and brighteft genius fing.
     The mufes' favourite pleas'd to live,
     Paying them back the fame they give.

IX.

But oh ! as greatly I afpire
   To tell my love, to fpeak thy praife,
Boafting no more its fprightly fire,
   My bofom heaves, my voice decays ;
     With pain I touch the mournful ftring
     And pant and languifh as I fing.

X.

Faint nature now demands that breath,
   Which feebly ftrives thy worth to fing !
And would be hufh'd and loft in death,
   Did not thy care kind fuccours bring !
     Thy pitying cafk my foul fuftain,
     And call new life in every vein.

XI.

The fober glafs I now behold,
  Thy health, with fair Francifca's join,
Wifhing her cheeks may long unfold
  Such beauties, and be ever thine ;
    No chance the tender joy remove,
    While fhe can pleafe, and thou canft love.

XII.

Thus while by you the Britifh arms
  Triumphs and diftant fame purfue ;
The yielding fair refigns her charms,
  And gives you leave to conquer too ;
    Her fnowy neck, her breaft, her eyes,
    And all the nymph becomes your prize.

XIII.

What comely grace, what beauty fmiles,
  Upon her lips what fweetnefs dwells ?
Not love himfelf fo oft beguiles,
  Nor Venus' felf fo much excells ;
    What different fates our paffions fhare
    While you enjoy, and I defpair ?

XIV.

* Maria's form as I furvey,
　Her fmiles a thoufand wounds impart;
Each feature fteals my foul away,
　Each glance deprives me of my heart.
　　And chacing thence each other fair,
　Leaves her own image only there.

XV.

Altho' my anxious breaft defpair,
　And fighing, hopes no kind return:
Yet for the lov'd relentlefs fair
　By night I wake, by day I burn.
　　Nor can thy gift foft fleep fupply,
　Or foothe my pains, or clofe my eye.

---

* Mrs. MARY MEERS, daughter to the principal of
Brazen-nofe.

THE

SPLENDID SHILLING:

AN

IMITATION

OF

MILTON.

——*Sing, heavenly muse,*
Things unattempted yet, in prose or rhime,
A Shilling, Breeches, and Chimeras dire.

HAPPY the man, who, void of cares and strife,
In silken, or in leathern, purse retains
A SPLENDID SHILLING: he nor hears with pain
New oysters cry'd, nor sighs for chearful ale;
But with his friends, when nightly mists arise,

To Juniper's Magpye, or Town-Hall * repairs :
Where, mindful of the nymph whose wanton eye
Transfix'd his soul, and kindled amorous flames,
Chloe, or Phillis ; he each circling glaſs
Wiſheth her health, and joy, and equal love.
Mean while, he ſmokes, and laughs at merry tale,
Or pun ambiguous, or conundrum quaint.
But I, whom griping penury ſurrounds,
And hunger, ſure attendant upon want,
With ſcanty offals, and ſmall acid tiff
(Wretched repaſt !) my meagre corps ſuſtain :
Then ſolitary walk, or doze at home
In garret vile, and with a warming puff
Regal chill'd fingers ; or from tube as black
As winter chimney, or well-poliſh'd jet,
Exhale Mundungus, ill-perfuming ſcent :
Not blacker tube, nor of a ſhorter ſize,
Smokes Cambro-Briton (vers'd in pedigree,
Sprung from Cadwalader and Arthur, kings
Full famous in romantic tale) when he
O'er many a craggy hill and barren cliff,
Upon a cargo of fam'd Ceſtrian cheeſe,
High over-ſhadowing rides, with a deſign
To vend his wares, or at th' Arvonian mart,
Or Maridunum, or the antient town
Yclip'd Brechinia, or where Vaga's ſtream
Encircles Ariçonium, faithful ſoil !

* Two noted ale-houſes in Oxford.

Herefordſhire

Whence flow nectareous wines, that well may vie
With Maffic, Setin, or renown'd Falern.
　　Thus, while my joylefs minutes tedious flow,
With looks demure, and filent pace, a Dun,
Horrible monfter! hated by gods and men,
To my aerial citadel afcends,
With vocal hael thrice thund'ring at my gate,
With hideous accent thrice he calls ; I know
The voice ill-boding and the folemn found.
What fhou'd I do ? or whither turn ? amaz'd,
Confounded, to the dark recefs I fly
Of woodhole ; ftrait my briftling hairs erect
Thro' fudden fear ; a chilly fweat bedews
My fhud'ring limbs, and (wonderful to tell !)
My tongue forgets her faculty of fpeech ;
So horrible he feems ! his faded brow
Entrench'd with many a frown, and conic beard,
And fpreading band, admir'd by modern faints,
Difaftrous acts forebode ; in his right hand
Long fcrolls of paper folemnly he waves,
With characters, and figures, dire infcrib'd,
Grievous to mortal eyes ; (ye gods ! avert
Such plagues from righteous men ;) behind him
Another monfter not unlike himfelf,　　(ftalks
Sullen of afpect, by the vulgar call'd
A Catchpole, whofe polluted hands the gods
With force incredible, and magic charms
Erft have undu'd ; if he his ample palm
Should haply on ill-fated fhoulder lay

Of debtor, ftrait his body, to the touch
Obfequious, (as whilom knights were wont)
To fome inchanted caftle is convey'd,
Where gates impregnable, and coercive chains
In durance ftri&t detain him, till in form
Of money, Pallas fets the captive free.

Beware, ye debtors, when ye walk beware,
Be circumfpe&t ; oft with infidious ken
This caitiff eyes your fteps aloof, and oft
Lies perdue in a nook or gloomy cave,
Prompt to inchant fome inadvertent wretch
With his unhallow'd touch.   So (poets fing)
Grimalkin to domeftic vermin fworn
An everlafting foe, with watchful eye
Lies nightly brooding o'er a chinky gap,
Protending her fell claws, to thoughtlefs mice
Sure ruin.   So her difembowel'd web
Arachne in a hall, or kitchen fpreads,
Obvious to vagrant flies : fhe fecret ftands
Within her woven cell; the humming prey,
Regardlefs of their fate, rufh on the toils
Inextricable, nor will aught avail
Their arts, or arms, or fhapes of lovely hue ;
The wafp infidious and the brazzing drone,
And butterfly proud of expanded wings,
Diftin&t with gold, entangled in her fnares,
Ufelefs refiftance make : with eager ftrides,
She tow'ring flies to her expe&ted fpoils ;

Then, with envenom'd jaws the vital blood
Drinks of reluctant foes, and to her cave
Their bulky carcaffes triumphant drags.
  So pafs my days.   But when nocturnal fhades
This world invelpp, and th' inclement air
Perfuades men to repel benumming frofts
With pleafant wines, and crackling blaze of wood;
Me lonely fitting, nor the glimmering light
Of make-weight candle, nor the joyous talk
Of loving friend delights ; diftrefs'd, forlorn,
Amidft the horrors of the tedious night,
Darkling I figh, and feed with difmal thoughts
My anxious mind ; or fometimes mournful verfe
Indite, and fing of groves and myrtle fhades,
Or defperate lady near a purling ftream,
Or lover pendent on a willow-tree.
Mean while I labour with eternal drought,
And reftlefs wifh, and rave ; my parched throat
Finds no relief, nor heavy eyes repofe :
But if a flumber haply does invade
My weary limbs, my fancy's ftill awake,
Thoughtful of drink, and eager, in a dream,
Tipples imaginary pots of ale,
In vain ; awake I find the fettled thirft
Still gnawing, and the pleafant fantom curfe.
  Thus do I live from pleafure quite debarr'd,
Nor tafte the fruits that the fun's genial rays
Mature, John-Apple, nor the downy Peach,

Nor Walnut in rough furrow'd coat secure,
Nor Medlar-fruit, delicious in decay :
Afflictions great ! yet greater still remain :
My Galligaskins that have long withstood
The winter's fury, and incroaching frosts,
By time subdu'd, (what will not time subdue !)
An horrid chasm disclose, with orifice,
Wide, discontinuous ; at which the winds
Eurus and Auster, and the dreadful force
Of Boreas, that congeals the Cronian waves,
Tumultuous enter with dire chilling blasts,
Portending agues. Thus a well fraught ship
Long sail'd secure, or thro' th' Ægean deep,
Or the Ionian, till cruising near
The Lilybean shore, with hideous crush
On Scylla, or Charibdis (dang'rous rocks !)
She strikes rebounding, whence the shatter'd oak,
So fierce a rock unable to withstand,
Admits the sea ; in at the gaping side
The crouding waves gush with impetuous rage,
Resistless, overwhelming ; horrors seize
The mariners, death in their eyes appears. (pray :
They stare, they lave, they pump, they swear, they
(Vain efforts !) still the battering waves rush in,
Implacable, till delug'd by the foam,
The ship sinks found'ring in the vast abyss.

BLEINHEIM:

A

POEM,

INSCRIBED TO THE RIGHT HONOURABLE

ROBERT HARLEY, Esq;

FROM low and abject themes the grov'ling
    Now mounts aerial to sing of arms   (muse
Triumphant, and emblaze the martial acts
Of Britain's hero ; may the verse not sink
Beneath his merits, but detain a while
Thy ear, O Harley ! (tho' thy country's weal
Depends on thee, tho' mighty ANNE requires
Thy hourly counsels) since with every art
Thyself adorn'd the mean essays of youth
Thou wilt not damp, but guide wherever found,
The willing genius to the muses seat :
Therefore the first, and last, the muse shall sing.
    Long had the Gallic monarch uncontroul'd
Enlarg'd his borders, and of human force

Opponent flightly thought, in heart elate,
As erft Sefoftris, (proud Ægyptian king,
That monarchs harnafs'd to his chariot yokt,
(Bafe fervitude!) and his dethron'd compeers
Lafh'd furious; they in fullen majefty
Drew the uneafy load.) Nor lefs he aim'd
At univerfal fway: for William's arm
Could nought avail, however fam'd in war;
Nor armies leagu'd, that diverfly aflay'd
To curb his power enormous; like an oak
That ftands fecure, tho' all the winds employ
Their ceafelefs rore, and only fheds its leaves,
Or maft, which the revolving fpring reftores:
So ftood he, and alone; alone defy'd
The European thrones combin'd, and ftill
Had fet at nought their machinations vain,
But that great Anne, weighing th' events of war
Momentous, in her prudent heart, thee chofe,
Thee, Churchill! to direct in nice extremes
Her banner'd legions. Now their priftine worth
The Britons recollect, and gladly change
Sweet native home for unaccuftom'd air,
And other climes, where diff'rent food and foil
Portend diftempers; over dank, and dry,
They journey toilfome, unfatigu'd with length
Of march, unftruck with horror at the fight
Of Alpine ridges black, high ftretching hills,
All white with fummer fnows. They go beyond

The trace of Englifh fteps, where fcarce the found
Of Henry's arms arriv'd ; fuch ftrength of heart
Thy conduct and example gives ; nor fmall   -
Encouragement, Godolphin, wife and juft,
Equal in merit, honour and fuccefs,
To Burleigh, (fortunate alike to ferve
The beft of queens :) he, of the royal ftore
Splendidly frugal, fits whole nights devoid
Of fweet repofe, induftrious to procure
The foldier's eafe ; to region far remote
His care extends, and to the Britifh hoft
Makes ravag'd countries plenteous as their own.

   And now, O Churchill! at thy wifh'd approach,
The-Germans hopelefs of fuccefs, forlorn,
With many an inroad gor'd, their drooping cheer
New animated roufe.   Not more rejoice
The miferable race of men, that live
Benighted half the year, benumb'd with frofts
Perpetual, and rough Boreas' keeneft breath,
Under the polar bear, inclement fky,
When firft the fun with new-born light removes
The long incumbent gloom.   Gladly to thee
Heroic laurel'd Eugene yields the prime,
Nor thinks it diminution, to be rank'd
In military honour next, altho'
His deadly hand fhook the Turcheftan throne
Accurs'd, and prov'd in far divided lands
Victorious ; on thy pow'rful fword alone

Germania, and the Belgic coaft relies,
Won from th' incroaching fea : that fword great
Fix'd not in vain on thy puiffant fide,   (ANNE
When thee fh' enroll'd her garter'd knights among,
Illuftrating the noble lift ; her hand
Affures good omens, and faint George's worth
Enkindles like defire of high exploits :
Immediate fieges, and the tire of war
Roll in thy eager mind ; thy plumy creft
Nods horrible, with more terrific port
Thou walk'ft, and feem'ft already in the fight.
  What fpoils, what conquefts then did Albion hope
From thy atchievements ! yet thou haft furpaft
Her boldeft vows, exceeded what thy foes
Could fear, or fancy ; they, in multitude
Superior, fed their thoughts with profpect vain
Of victory and rapine, reck'ning what
From ranfom'd captives would accrue. Thus one
Jovial his mate befpoke ; O friend ! obferve,
How gay with all th' accoutrements of war (come
The Britons come, with gold well fraught they
Thus far, our prey, and tempt us to fubdue
Their recreant force ; how will their bodies ftript
Enrich the victors, while the vultures fate
Their maws with full repaft ! Another, warm'd
With high ambition, and conceit of prowefs
Inherent, arrogantly thus prefum'd :
What if this fword, full often drench'd in blood
Of bafe antagonifts, with griding edge

Should now cleave fheer the execrable head
Of Churchill, met in arms! or if this hand,
Soon as his army difarray'd 'gins fwerve,
Should ftay him flying with retentive gripe,
Confounded, and appal'd! no trivial price
Should fet him free, nor fmall fhould be my praife
To lead him fhackled, and expofe to fcorn,
Of gath'ring crouds the Briton's boafted chief.

   Thus they, in fportive mood, their empty taunts
And menaces exprefs'd; nor could their prince
In arms, vain Tallard, from opprobrious fpeech
Refrain: Why halt ye thus, ye Britons? why
Decline the war? Shall a morafs forbid
Your eafy march? Advance; we'll bridge a way,
Safe of accefs. Imprudent, thus t' invite
A furious lion to his folds! that boaft
He ill abides, captiv'd in other plight
He foon revifits Brittany, that once
Refplendent came, with ftretcht retinue girt,
And pompous pageantry: O haplefs fate,
If any arm, but Churchill's had prevail'd!

   No need fuch boafts, or exprobations falfe
Of cowardice; the military mound
The Britifh files tranfcend, in evil hour
For their proud foes that fondly brav'd their fate.
And now on either fide the trumpet blew,
Signal of-onfet, refolution firm
Infpiring, and pernicious love of war.

The adverfe fronts in rueful conflict meet,
Collecting all their might; for on th' event
Decifive of this bloody day depends
The fate of kingdoms: with lefs vehemence
The great competitors for Rome engag'd,
Cæfar, and Pompey; on Pharfalian plains,
Where ftern Bellona, with one final ftroke,
Adjudg'd the empire of this globe to one.
Here the Bavarian duke his brigades leads,
Gallant in arms, aud gaudy to behold,
Bold champion ! brandifhing his Noric blade,
Beft temper'd fteel, fuccefslefs prov'd in field !
Next Tallard, with his Celtic infantry (prompt
Prefumptuous comes : here Churchill, not fo
To vaunt, as fight, his hardy cohorts joins
With Eugene's German force. Now from each van
The brazen inftruments of death difcharge
Horrible flames, and turbid ftreaming clouds
Of fmoke fulphureous ; intermix'd with thefe
Large globus irons fly, of dreadful hifs,
Singing the air, and from long diftance bring
Surprizing flaughter ; on each fide they fly
By chains connext, and with deftructive fweep
Behead whole troops at once ; the hairy fcalps
Are whirl'd aloof, while numerous trunks beftrow
Th' enfanguin'd field ; with latent mifchief ftor'd
Showers of granadoes rain, by fudden burft
Difploding murd'rous bowels, fragments of fteel,
And ftones, and glafs, and nitrous grain aduft.

A thoufand ways at once the fhiver'd orbs
Fly diverfe, working torment, and foul rout
With deadly bruife, and gafhes furrow'd deep.
Of pain impatient, the high prancing fteeds
Difdain the curb, and flinging to and fro,
Spurn their difmounted riders ; they expire
Indignant, by unhoftile wounds deftroy'd.

Thus thro' each army death, in various fhapes,
Prevail'd; here mangled limbs, here brains and gore
Lie clotted; lifelefs fome : with anguifh thefe
Gnafhing, and loud laments invoking aid,
Unpity'd, and unheard ; the louder din
Of guns, and trumpets clang, and folemn found
Of drums, o'ercame their groans. In equal fcale
Long hung the fight, few marks of fear were feen,
None of retreat : as when two adverfe winds,
Sublim'd from dewy vapours, in mid fky
Engage with horrid fhock, the ruffled brine
Roars ftormy, they together dafh the clouds,
Levying their equal force with utmoft rage ;
Long undecided lafts the airy ftrife.

So they, incens'd: 'till Churchill, viewing where
The violence of Tallard moft prevail'd,
Came to oppofe his flaught'ring arm ; with fpeed
Precipitant he rode, urging his way
O'er hills of gafping heroes, and fall'n fteeds
Rolling in death : deftruction, grim with blood,
Attends his furious courfe. Him thus enrag'd
Defcrying from afar fome engineer,

Dextrous to guide the unerring charge, defign'd
By one nice fhot to terminate the war.
With aim direct the levell'd bullet flew,
But mifs'd her fcope (for deftiny withftood
Th' approaching wound) and guiltlefs plough'd her
Beneath his courfer; round his facred head　(way
The glowing balls play innocent, while he
With dire impetuous fway deals fatal blows,
Amongft the fcatter'd Gauls.　But O! beware,
Great warrior, nor too prodigal of life
Expofe the Britifh fafety: hath not Jove
Already warn'd thee to withdraw! Referve
Thyfelf for other palms.　Ev'n now thy aid.
Eugene, with regiments unequal preft,
Awaits: this day of all his honours gain'd
Defpoils him, if thy fuccour opportune
Defends not the fad hour: permit not thou
So brave a leader with the vulgar herd
To bite the ground unnoted——Swift, and fierce
As wintry ftorm, he flies, to reinforce
The yielding wing; in Gallic blood again
He dews his reeking fword, and ftrews the ground
With headlefs ranks; (fo Ajax interpos'd
His feven-fold fhield, and fkreen'd Laertes' fon,
For valour much, and warlike wiles renown'd,
When the infulting Trojans urg'd him fore
With tilted fpears :) unmanly dread invades
The French aftony'd; ftraight their ufelefs arms
They quit, and in their fwift retreat confide,

Unfeemly yelling ; diftant hills return
The hideous noife.   What can they do ? or, how
Withftand his wide deftroying fword ? or where
Find fhelter thus repuls'd ? Behind with wrath
Refiftlefs, th' eager Englifh champions prefs,
Chaftifing tardy flight ; before them rolls,
His current fwift the Danube, vaft, and deep,
Supream of rivers ; to the frightful brink,
Urg'd by compulfive arms, foon as they reach'd,
New horror chill'd their veins ; devote they faw
Themfelves to wretched doom ; with efforts vain,
Encourag'd by defpair, or obftinate
To fall like men in arms, fome dare renew.
Feeble engagement, meeting glorious fate
On the firm land ; the reft difcomfited,
And pufh'd by Marlborough's avengeful hand,
Leap plunging in the wide extended flood :
Bands, numerous as the Memphian foldiery
That fwell'd the Erythræan wave, when wall'd
The unfroze waters marvelloufly ftood,
Obfervant of the great command.   Upbore
By frothy billows thoufands float the ftream
In cumbrous mail, with love of farther fhore ;
Confiding in their hands, that fed'lous ftrive
To cut th' outragious fluent : in this diftrefs
Ev'n in the fight of death, fome, tokens fhew
Of fearlefs friendfhip, and their finking mates
Suftain ; vain love, tho' laudable ! abforpt
By a fierce eddy, they together found

The vaft profundity; their horfes paw
The fwelling furge, with fruitlefs toil: furcharg'd,
And in his courfe obftrueted by large fpoil,
The river flows redundant, and attacks
The ling'ring remnant with unufual tide;
Then rolling back, in his capacious lap
Ingulfs their whole militia, quick immerft.
So when fome fwelt'ring travellers retire
To leafy fhades, near the cool funlefs verge
Of Paraba, Brafilian ftream; her tail
Of vaft extenfion, from her watry den,
A grifly Hydra fuddenly fhoots forth,
Infidious, and with curl'd invenom'd train
Embracing horridly, at once the crew
Into the river whirles; th' unweeting prey
Entwifted roars, the parted wave rebounds.
　　Nor did the Britifh fquadrons now furceafe
To gall their foes o'erwhelm'd; full many felt
In the moift element a fcorching death,
Pierc'd finking; fhrouded in a dufky cloud
The current flows, with livid miffive flames
Boiling, as once Pergamian Xanthus boil'd,
Inflam'd by Vulcan, when the fwift-footed fon
of Peleus to his baleful banks purfu'd
The ftraggling Trojans: Nor lefs eager drove
Viétorious Churchill his defponding foes
Into the deep immenfe, that many a league
Impurpled ran, with gufhing gore diftain'd.

Thus the experienc'd valour of one man,
Mighty in conflict, refcu'd harraſt pow'rs
From ruin impendent, and th' afflicted throne
Imperial, that once lorded o'er the world,
Suſtain'd. With prudent ſtay, he long deferr'd
The rough contention, nor would deign to rout
An hoſt diſparted ; when, in union firm
Embody'd, they advanc'd, collecting all
Their ſtrength, and worthy ſeem'd to be ſubdu'd;
He the proud boaſters ſent, with ſtern aſſault,
Down to the realms of night. The Britiſh ſouls,
(A lamentable race !) that ceas'd to breathe,
On Landen-plains, this heav'nly gladſome air,
Exult to ſee the crouding ghoſts deſcend
Unnumber'd ; well aveng'd, they quit the cares
Of mortal life, and drink th' oblivious lake.
Not ſo the new inhabitants : They roam
Erroneous, and diſconſolate, themſelves
Accuſing, and their chiefs, improvident
Of military chance ; when lo ! they ſee,
Thro' the dun miſt, in blooming beauty freſh,
Two lovely youths, that amicably walkt
O'er verdant meads, and pleas'd, perhaps, revolv'd
Anna's late conqueſts ; one, to empire born,
Egregious prince ! whoſe manly childhood ſhew'd
His mingled parents, and portended joy
Unſpeakable ; thou, his aſſociate dear
Once in this world, nor now by fate disjoined,
Had thy preſiding ſtar propitious ſhone,

Shouldſt Churchill be! but heaven ſevere cut ſhort
Their ſpringing years, nor would this iſle ſhould
Gifts ſo important! Them the Gallic ſhades (boaſt
Surveying, read in either radiant look
Marks of exceſſive dignity and grace,
Delighted; till, in one, their curious eye
Diſcerns their great ſubduer's awful mein,
And correſponding features fair; to them
Confuſion! ſtraight the airy phantoms fleet,
With headlong haſte, and dread a new purſuit.
The image pleas'd with joy paternal ſmiles.

    Enough, O muſe! the ſadly pleaſing theme
Leave, with theſe dark abodes, and re-aſcend
To breathe the upper air where triumphs wait
The conq'ror, and ſav'd nations joint acclaim.
Hark! how the cannon, inoffenſive now,
Give ſigns of gratulation; ſtruggling crouds
From every city flow; with ardent gaze
Fixt, they behold the Britiſh guide, of ſight
Inſatiate, whilſt his great redeeming hand
Each prince affects to touch reſpectful. See,
How Pruſſia's king tranſported entertains
His mighty gueſt; to him the royal pledge,
Hope of his realm, commits, (with better fate,
Than to the Trojan chief Evander gave
Unhappy Pallas) and intreats to ſhew
The ſkill and rudiments auſtere of war.
See, with what joy, him Leopold declares
His great deliverer; and courts t' accept

Of titles, with superior modesty
Better refus'd.   Mean while the haughty king
Far humbler thoughts now learns; despair, and fear
Now first he feels; his laurels all at once
Torn from his aged head, in life's extreme,
Distract his soul; nor can great Boileau's harp
Of various sounding wire, best taught to claim
Whatever passion, and exalt the soul
With highest strains, his languid spirits cheer:
Rage, shame, and grief, alternate in his breast.
    But who can tell what pangs, what sharp remorse
Torment the Boian prince? From native soil
Exil'd by fate, torn from the dear embrace
Of weeping consort, and depriv'd the sight
Of his young guiltless progeny, he seeks
Inglorious shelter, in an alien land;
Deplorable! but that his mind averse
To right, and insincere, would violate
His plighted faith: why did he not accept
Friendly composure offer'd? or well weigh,
With whom he must contend? Encount'ring fierce
The Solymæan sultan, he o'erthrew
His moony troops, returning bravely smear'd
With painim blood effus'd; nor did the Gaul
Not find him once a baleful foe: but when,
Of council rash, new measures he pursues,
Unhappy prince! (no more a prince, he sees
Too late his error, forc'd t'implore relief

F

Of him, he once defy'd.   O deftitute
Of hope, unpity'd! thou fhould'ft firft have thought
Of perfevering ftedfaft; now upbraid
Thy own inconftant ill-afpiring heart.
Lo! how the Noric plains, thro' thy default,
Rife hilly, with large piles of flaughter'd knights,
Beft men, that warr'd ftill firmly for their prince,
Tho' faithlefs, and unfhaken duty fhew'd:
Worthy of better end.   Where cities ftood,
Well fenc'd, and numerous, defolation reigns,-
And emptinefs, difmay'd, unfed, unhous'd,
The widow and the orphan ftrole around
The defart wide; with oft retorted eye
They view the gaping walls, and poor remains
Of manfions, once their own (now loathfome
Of birds obfcene,) bewailing loud the lofs (haunts
Of fpoufe, or fire, or fon, ere manly prime
Slain in fad conflict, and complain of fate
As partial, and too rigorous; nor find
Where to retire themfelves, or where appeafe
Th' afflictive keen defire of food, expos'd
To winds, and ftorms, and jaws of favage beafts.
    Thrice happy Albion! from the world disjoin'd
By heaven propitious, blefsful feat of peace!
Learn from thy neighbour's miferies to prize
Thy welfare; crown'd with nature's choiceft gifts,
Remote thou hear'ft the dire effect of war,
Depopulation, void alone of fear,
And peril, whilft the difmal fymphony

Of drums and clarions other realms annoys.
Th' Iberian fcepter undecided, here
Engages mighty hofts in wafteful ftrife ;
From different climes the flower of youth defcends
Down to the Lufitanian vales, refolv'd
With utmoft hazard to enthrone their prince,
Gallic, or Auftrian ; havoc dire enfues,
And wild uproar : the natives dubious whom
They muft obey, in confternation wait,
'Till rigid conqueft will pronounce their liege.
Nor is the brazen voice of war unheard
On the mild Latian fhore : what fighs and tears
Hath Eugene caus'd ! How many widows curfe
His cleaving faulchion ! Fertile foil in vain !
What do thy paftures, or thy vines avail,
Beft boon of heaven ! or huge Taburnus, cloth'd
With olives, when the cruel battle mows
The planters, with their harveft immature ?
See, with what outrage from the frofty north,
The early valiant Swede draws forth his wings
In batailous array, while Volga's ftream
Sends oppofite, in fhaggy armour clad,
Her borderers ; on mutual flaughter bent,
They rend their countries. How is Poland vext
With civil broils, while two elected kings
Contend for fway ? Unhappy nation, left
Thus free of choice ! The Englifh undifturb'd
With fuch fad privilege, fubmifs obey -   (due,
Whom heaven ordains fupreme, with rev'rence

Not thraldom, in fit liberty fecure.
From fcepter'd kings, in long defcent deriv'd,
Thou Anna ruleft, prudent to promote
Thy people's eafe at home, nor ftudious lefs
Of Europe's good ; to thee, of kingly rights
Sole arbitrefs, declining thrones,.and powers,
Sue for relief ; thou bid'ft thy Churchill go, -
Succour the injur'd realms, defeat the hopes.
Of haughty Louis, unconfin'd ; he goes
Obfequious, and the dread command fulfils,
In one great day.   Again thou giv'ft in charge
To Rook, that he fhould let that monarch know,
The empire of the ocean wide diffus'd
Is thine ; behold ! with winged fpeed he rides
Undaunted o'er the lab'ring main t' affert
Thy liquid kingdoms ; at his near approach
The Gallic navy impotent to bear
His volly'd thunder, torn, diffever'd, fcud,
And blefs the friendly interpofing night.

    Hail, mighty Queen ! referv'd by fate, to grace
The new-born age ; what hopes may we conceive
Of future years, when to thy early reign
Neptune fubmits his trident, and thy arms
Already have prevail'd to th' utmoft bound,
Hefperian, Calpe, by Alcides fixt,
Mountain fublime, that cafts a fhade of length
Immeafurable, and rules the inland waves !
Let others, with infatiate thirft of rule,
Invade their neighbours lands, negleft the ties

Of leagues and oaths; this thy peculiar praife
Be ftill, to ftudy right, and quell the force
Of kings perfidious; let them learn from thee
That neither ftrength, nor policy refin'd,
Shall with fuccefs be crown'd, where juftice fails.
Thou with thy own content, not for thyfelf,
Subdueft regions; generous to raife
The fuppliant knee, and curb the rebel neck.
The German boafts thy conquefts, and enjoys
The great advantage; nought to thee redounds
But fatisfaction from thy confcious mind.

   Aufpicious Queen! fince in rhy realms fecure
Of peace, thou reign'ft, and victory attends
Thy diftant enfigns, with compaffion view
Europe embroil'd; ftill thou (for thou alone
Sufficient art) the jarring kingdoms ire.
Reciprocally ruinous; fay who.
Shall wield th' Hefperian, who the Polifh fword,
By thy decree; the trembling lands fhall hear
Thy voice, obedient, left thy fcourge fhould bruife
Their ftubborn necks, and Churchill in his wrath
Make them remember Bleinheim with regret.

   Thus fhall the nations, aw'd to peace, extol
Thy pow'r, and juftice; jealoufies and fears,
And hate infernal banifh'd fhall retire
To Mauritania, or the Bactrian coafts,
Or Tartary, engend'ring difcords fell
Among the enemies of truth; while arts

Pacific, and inviolable love
Flourifh in Europe.   Hail Saturnian days
Returning! In perpetual tenor run
Dele&table, and fhed your influence fweet
On virtuous Anna's head; ye happy days,
By her reftor'd, her juft defigns compleat,
And, mildly on her fhining, blefs the world !

 Thus from the noify croud exempt, with eafe,
And plenty bleft, amid the mazy groves;
Sweet folitude ! where warb'ling birds provoke
The filent mufe, delicious rural feat
Of Saint John, Englifh Memmius, I prefum'd
To fing Britannic trophies, inexpert
Of war, with mean attempt ; while he intent
(So Anna's will ordains) to expedite
His military charge, * no leifure finds
To ftring his charming fhell; but when return'd
Confummate peace fhall rear her chearful head,
Then fhall his Churchill in fublimer verfe
For ever triumph ; lateft times fhall learn,
From fuch a Chief to fight, and Bard to fing.

   * He was then fecretary of war.

C · Y · D E R.

B O O K I.

——*Honos erit huic quoque Pomo ?*　　VIRG.

WHAT foil the apple loves, what care is due
　　To orchats, timelieft when to prefs the
Thy gift, Pomona! in Miltonian verfe 　(fruits,
Adventrous I prefume to fing ; of verfe
Nor fkill'd nor ftudious : but my native foil
Invites me, and the theme as yet unfung.
　Ye Ariconian knights, and faireft dames,
To whom propitious heaven thofe bleffings grants,
Attend my lays ; nor hence difdain to learn,
How nature's gifts may be improv'd by art.
　And thou, O Moyftin! whofe benevolence,
And candour, oft experienc'd, me vouchfaf'd
To knit in friendfhip, growing ftill with years,
Accept this pledge of gratitude and love.
May it a lafting monument remain
Of dear refpect ; that, when this body frail
Is moulder'd into duft, and I become

As I had never been, late times may know
I once was blefs'd in fuch a matchlefs friend.
Who e'er expects his lab'ring trees fhould bend
With fruitage, and a kindly harveft yield,
Be this his firft concern ; to find a tract
Impervious to the winds, begirt with hills,
That intercept the Hyperborean blafts
Tempeftuous, aud cold Eurus' nipping force,
Noxius to feeble buds : but to the weft
Let him free entrance grant; let Zephyrs bland
Adminifter their tepid genial airs ;
Naught fear he from the weft, whofe gentle warmth
Difclofes well the earth's all-teeming womb,
Invigorating tender feeds : whofe breath
Nurtures the Orange, and the Citron groves,
Hefperian fruits, and wafts their odours fweet
Wide thro' the air, and diftant fhores perfumes.
Nor only do the hills exclude the winds :
But, when the black'ning clouds in fprinkling fhow'rs
Diftill, from the high fummits down the rain
Runs trickling ; with the fertile moifture chear'd,
The orchats fmile ; joyous the farmers fee
Their thriving plants, and blefs the heavenly dew.
Next, let the planter, with difcretion meet,
The force and genius of each foil explore ;
To what adapted, what it fhuns averfe :
Without this neceffary care, in vain
He hopes an apple-vintage, and invokes

Pomona's aid in vain. The miry fields,
Rejoicing in rich mold, moft ample fruit
Of beauteous form produce: pleafing to fight,
But to the tongue inelegant and flat.
So nature has decreed; fo, oft we fee
Men paffing fair, in outward lineaments
Elaborate, lefs, inwardly, exact.
Nor from the fable ground expect fuccefs,
Nor from cretaceous, ftubborn and jejune:
The muft, of pallid hue, declares the foul
Devoid of fpirit; wretched he, that quaffs
Such wheyifh liquors; oft with colic pangs,
With pungent colic pangs diftrefs'd, he'll roar,
And tofs, and turn, and curfe th' unwholefome draught.
But, farmer, look, where full-ear'd fheaves of rye
Grow wavy on the tilth, that foil felect
For apples; thence thy induftry fhall gain
Ten-fold reward; thy garners, thence with ftore
Surcharg'd, fhall burft; thy prefs with pureft juice
Shall flow, which, in revolving years, may try
Thy feeble feet, and bind thy fault'ring tongue.
Such is the Kentchurch, fuch Danzeyan ground,
Such thine, O learned Brome! and Caple fuch,
Willifian Burlton, much-lov'd Geers his Marfh,
And Sutton-acres, drench'd with regal blood
Of Ethelbert, when to th'unhallow'd feaft
Of Mercian Offa he invited came,
To treat of fpoufals: long connubial joys

He promis'd to himfelf, allur'd by fair
Elfrida's beauty ; but deluded dy'd
In height of hopes——Oh ! hardeft fate, to fall
By fhew of friendfhip, and pretended love !
  I nor advife, nor apprehend the choice
Of Marcely-hill ; the apple no where finds
A kinder mold : yet 'tis unfafe to truft
Deceitful ground : who knows, but that once more,
This mount may journey, and, his prefent fite
Forfaking, to thy neighbours bounds transfer
the goodly plants, affording matter ftrange
For law-debates ! If, therefore, thou incline
To deck this rife with fruits of various taftes,
Fail not by frequent vows to implore fuceefs ;
Thus piteous heaven may fix the wand'ring glebe.
  But if (for nature doth not fhare alike
Her gifts) an happy foil fhould be with-held ;
If a penurious clay fhould be thy lot,
Or rough unwieldy earth, nor to the plough,
Nor to the cattle kind, with fandy ftones
And gravel o'er-abounding, think it not
Beneath thy toil ; the fturdy pear-tree here
Will rife luxuriant, and with tougheft root
Pierce the obftruding grit, and reftive marle.
This naught is ufelefs made ; nor is there land,
But what, or of itfelf, or elfe compell'd,
Affords advantage. On the barren heath
The fhepherd tends his ftock, that daily crop

Their vardant dinner from the moffie turf,
Sufficient ; after them the crackling goofe,
Clofe-grazer, finds wherewith to eafe her want.
What fhould I more ? Even on the cliffy height
Of Penmenmaur, and that cloud-piercing hill,
Plinlimmon, from afar the traveller kens
Aftonifh'd, how the goats their fhrubby brouze
Gnaw pendent ; nor untrembling canft thou fee
How from a fcraggy rock, whofe prominence
Half overfhades the ocean, hardy men,
Fearlefs of rending winds, and dafhing waves,
Cut famphire, to excite the fqueamifh guft
Of pamper'd luxury.   Then, let thy ground
Not lye unlabour'd ; if the richeft ftem
Refufe to thrive, yet who would doubt to plant
Somewhat, that may to human ufe redound,
And penury, the worft of ills, remove ?
There are, who, fondly ftudious of increafe,
Rich foreign mold on their ill-natur'd land
Induce laborious, and with fat'ning muck
Befmear the roots ; in vain ! the nurfling grove
Seems fair a while, cherifh'd with fofter earth :
But, when the alien compoft is exhauft,
Its native property again prevails.

    Tho' this art fails, defpond not ; little pains,
In a dew hour employ'd, great profit yield.
Th' induftrious when the fun in Leo rides,
And darts his fultrieft beams, portending drought,

Forgets not at the foot of ev'ry plant
To fink a circling trench, and daily pour
A juft fupply of aliemental ftreams,
Exhaufted fap recruiting ; elfe, falfe hopes
He cherifhes, nor will his fruit expeét
Th' autumnal feafon, but, in fummer's pride,
When other orchat's fmile, abortive fail.

Thus the great light of heaven that in his courfe
Surveys and quickens all things, often proves
Noxious to planted fields, and often men
Perceive his influence dire ; fwelt'ring they run
To grots, and caves, and the cool umbrage feek
Of woven arborets, and oft the rills
Still ftreaming frefh revifit, to allay
Thirft inextinguifhable : but if the fpring
Preceding fhould be deftitute of rain,
Or blaft feptentrional with' brufhing wings
Sweep up the fmoaky mifts, and vapours damp,
Then wo to mortals ! Titan then exerts
His heat intenfe, and on our vitals preys ;
Then maladies of various kinds, and names un-
Unknown, malignant fevers, and that foe (known,
To blooming beauty, which imprints the face
Of faireft nymph, and checks our growing love,
Reigns far and near ; grim death, in diff'rent
Depopulates the nations, thoufands fall (fhapes,
His victims, youths, and virgins, in their flower,
Reluctant die, and fighing leave their loves

Unfinifh'd, by infectious heaven deftroy'd.

Such heats prevail'd, when fair Eliza, laft
Of Winchcomb's name (next thee in blood, and
O faireft St. John!) left this toilfome world (worth,
In beauty's prime, and fadden'd all the year :
Nor could her virtues, nor repeated vows
Of thoufand lovers, the relentlefs hand -
Of death arreft ; fhe with the vulgar fell,
Only diftinguifh'd by this humble verfe.

But if it pleafe the fun's intemp'rate force
To know, attend ; whilft I of antient fame
The annals trace, and image to thy mind,
How our fore-fathers, (lucklefs men !) ingulft
By the wide yawning earth, to Stygian fhades
Went quick, in one fad fepulchre enclos'd.

In elder days, ere yet the Roman bands
Victorious, this our other world fubdu'd,
A fpacious city ftood, with firmeft walls
Sure mounded, and with num'rous turrets crown'd,
Aerial fpires, and citadels, the feat
Of kings, and heroes refolute in war,
Fam'd Ariconium ; uncontroul'd and free,
'Till all-fubduing Latian arms prevail'd.
Then alfo, tho' to foreign yoke fubmifs,
She undemolifh'd ftood, and even till now
Perhaps had ftood, of antient Britifh art
A pleafing monument, not lefs admir'd

G

Than what from Attic, or Etruscan hands
Arose; had not the heavenly powers averse
Decreed her final doom : for now the fields
Labour'd with thirst, Aquarius had not shed
His wonted showers, and Sirius parch'd with heat
Solstitial the green herb : hence 'gan relax
The ground's contexture, hence Tartarean dregs,
Sulphur, and nitrous spume, enkindling fierce,
Bellow'd within their darksome caves, by far
More dismal than the loud disploded roar
Of brazen engin'ry, that ceaseless storm
The bastion of a well built city, deem'd
Impregnable : th' infernal winds, 'till now
Closely imprison'd, by Titanian warmth,
Dilating, and with unctuous vapours fed,
Disdain'd their narrow cells ; and, their full
Collecting, from beneath the solid mass (strength
Unheav'd, and all her castles rooted deep
Shook from their lowest seats ; old Vaga's stream.
Forc'd by the sudden shock, her wonted tract
Forsook, and drew her humid train aslope,
Crankling her banks : and now the low'ring sky,
And baleful light'ning, and the thunder, voice
of angry gods, that rattled solemn, dismaid (turn
The sinking hearts of men. Where should they
Distress'd! whence seek for aid? when from below
Hell threatens, and even fate supreme gives signs
Of wrath and desolation ? Vain were vows,

And plaints, and fuppliant hands to heaven erect!
Yet fome to fanes repair'd, and humbler rites
Perform'd to Thor, and Woden, fabled gods,
Who with their vot'ries in one ruin fhar'd, (mood,
Crufh'd and o'erwhelm'd.   Others in frantic
Run howling thro' the ftreets; their hideous yells
Rend the dark welkin ; horror ftalks around,
Wild-ftaring, and, his fad concomitant,
Defpair of abject look : at every gate
The thronging populace with hafty ftrides
Prefs furious, and too eager of efcape,
Obftruct the eafy way ; the rocking town
Supplants their footfteps ; to and fro, they reel
Aftonifh'd, as o'er-charg'd with wine ; when lo
The ground aduft her riven mouth difparts,
Horrible chafm ; profound ! with fwift defcent
Old Ariconium finks, and all her tribes,
Heroes, and fenators, down to the realms
Of endlefs night. Mean-while, the loofen'd winds
Infuriate, molten rocks and flaming globes
Hurl'd high above the clouds ; 'till, all their force
Confum'd, her rav'nous jaws th' earth fatiate clos'd.
Thus this fair city fell, of which the name
Survives alone ; nor is there found a mark,
Whereby the curious paffenger may learn
Her ample fite, fave coins, and mould'ring urns,
And huge unweildy bones, lafting remains

Of that gigantic race ; which, as he breaks
The clotted glebe, the plowman haply finds,
Appall'd.   Upon that treacherous tract of land,
She whilome stood ; now Ceres, in her prime,
Smiles fertile, and with ruddieft freight bedeck'd,
The apple-tree, by our fore-fathers blood
Improv'd, that now recals the devious mufe,
Urging her deftin'd labours to purfue.

     The prudent will obferve, what paffions reign
In varicus plants (for not to man alone,
But all the wide creation, nature gave
Love and averfion) : everlafting hate
The Vine to Ivy bears, nor lefs abhors
The Coleworts ranknefs ; but, with amorous twine,
Clafps the tall Elm : the Pæftan Rofe unfolds
Her bud, more lovely, near the fetid Leek
(Creft of ftout Britons !) and inhances thence
The price of her celeftial fcent : the Gourd,
And thirfty Cucumber, when they perceive
Th' approaching Olive, with refentment fly
Her fatty fibres, and with tendrils creep
Diverfe, detefting contact ; while the Fig
Contemns not Rue, nor Sage's humble leaf,
Clofe neighbouring : the Herefordian plant
Careffes freely the contiguous Peach,
Hazel, and weight-refifting Palm, and likes
T' approach the Quince, and th' Elder's pithy
Uneafy, feated by funeral Yeugh,   (ftem,

Of Walnut, (whofe malignant touch impairs
All generous fruits,) or near the bitter dews
Of Cherries.   Therefore, weigh the habits well
Of plants, how they affociate beft, nor let
Ill neighbourhood corrupt thy hopeful grafs. (froth?
   Wouldft thou, thy vats with gen'rous juice fhould
Refpect thy orchats ; think not, that the trees
Spontaneous will produce an wholefome draught,
Let art correct thy breed : from parent bough
 A cyon meetly fever ; after, force
A way unto the crabftock's clofe-wrought grain
By wedges, and within the living wound
Enclofe the fofter twig ; nor over-nice
Refufe with thy own hands around to fpread
The binding clay : ere long their differing veins
Unite, and kindly nourifhment convey
To the new pupil; now he fhoots his arms (trunk,
With quickeft growth; now fhake the teeming
Down rain th'impurpled balls, ambrofial fruit.
Whether the Wilding's fibres are contriv'd
To draw the earth's pureft fpirit, and refift
Its feculence, which in more porous ftocks
Of Cyder-plants find paffage free, or elfe
The native verjuice of the Crab, deriv'd
Thro' th' infix'd graff, a grateful mixture forms
Of tart and fweet; whatever be the caufe,
This doubtful progeny by niceft taftes

G 3

Expected beft acceptance finds, and pays
Largeft revenues to the orchat-lord.
　Some think, the Quince and Apple would com-
In happy union ; others fittet deem 　　　 (bine
The Sloe-ftem bearing fylvan plumbs auftere.
Who knows but both may thrive ? Howe'er, what
To try the pow'ers of both, and fearch how far (lofs
Two different natures may concur to mix
In clofe embraces, and ftrange offspring bear ?
Thou'lt find that plants will frequent changes try,
Undamag'd, and their marriageable arms
Conjoin with others. 　So Silurian plants
Admit the Peach's odoriferous globe,
And pears of fundry forms ; at diff'rent times
Adopted Plumbs will alien branches grace ;
And men have gather'd from the Hawthorn's
Large Medlars, imitating regal crowns. 　(branch
　　Nor is it hard to beautify each month
With files of parti-colour'd fruits, that pleafe
The tongue, and view, at once. So Maro's mufe,
Thrice facred mufe ! commodious precepts gives
Inftructive to the fwains, not wholly bent
On what is gainful : fometimes fhe diverts
From folid counfels : fhews the force of love
In favage beafts ; how virgin face divine
Attracts the haplefs youth thro' ftorms and waves,
Alone, in deep of night : then fhe defcribes ‚
The Scythian winter, nor difdains to fing

How under ground the rude Riphœan race
Mimic brifk Cyder with the brakes product wild ;
Sloes pounded, hips, and Servis' harfheft juice.
    Let fage experience teach us all the arts
Of grafting, and in-eying ; when to lop
The flowing branches ; what trees anfwer beft
From root, or kernel : fhe will beft the hours
Of harveft, and feed-time declare ; by her
The diff'rent qualities of things were found,
And fecret motions ; how with heavy bulk
Volatile Hermes, fluid and unmoift,
Mounts on the wings of air ; to her we owe
The Indian weed, unknown to antient times,
Natures choice gift, whofe acrimonious fume
Extracts fuperfluous juices, and refines
The blood diftemper'd from its noxious falts ;
Friend to the fpirits, which with vapours bland
It gently mitigates, companion fit
Of pleafantry, and wine ; nor to the bards
Unfriendly, when they to the vocal fhell
Warble melodious their well-labour'd fongs.
She found the polifh'd glafs whofe fmall convex
Enlarges to ten millions of degrees
The mite, invifible elfe, of nature's hand
Left animal : and fhews, what laws of life
The cheefe-inhabitants obferve, and how
Fabric their manfions in the harden'd milk,
Wonderful artifts ! but the hidden ways

Of nature wouldft thou know? How firft fhe
All things in miniature? thy'fpecular orb (frames
Apply to well-diffected kernels; lo!
Strange forms arife, in each a little plant
Unfolds its boughs: obferve the flender threads
Of firft beginning trees, their roots, their leaves,
In narrow feeds defcrib'd; thou't wond'ring fay,
An inmate orchat ev'ry apple boafts.
Thus all things by experience are difplay'd,
And moft improv'd. Then feduloufly think
To meliorate thy ftock; no way, or rule,
Be unaffay'd; prevent the morning ftar
Affiduous, nor with the weftern fun
Surceafe to work. Lo! thoughtful of thy gain,
Not of my own, I all the live long day
Confume in meditation deep, reclufe
From human converfe, nor, at fhut of eve,
Enjoy repofe; but oft at midnight lamp
Ply my brain-racking ftudies, if by chance
Thee I may counfel right; and oft this care
Difturbs me flumb'ring. Wilt thou then repine
To labour for thyfelf? and rather chufe
To lye fupinely, hoping heaven will blefs
Thy flighted fruits, and give thee bread unearn'd?
'Twill profit, when the ftork, fworn-foe of
Returns, to fhew compaffion to thy plants, (fnakes,
Fatigu'd with breeding. Let the arched knife
Well fharpen'd now affail the fpreading fhades

Of vegetables, and their thirfty limbs
Diffever : for the genial moifture, due
To apples otherwife mifpends itfelf
In barren twigs, and for th' expected crop,
Naught but vain fhoots, and empty leaves abound.

　　When fwelling buds their od'rous foilage fhed,
And gently harden into fruit, the wife
Spare not the little off-fpring, if they grow
Redundant; but the thronging clufters thin
By kind avulfion : elfe, the ftarv'ling brood,
Void of fufficient fuftenance, will yield
A flender autumn ; which the niggard foul
Too late fhall weep, and curfe his thrifty hand,
That would not timely eafe the pond'rous boughs.

　　It much conduces, all the cares to know
Of gard'ning, how to fcare nocturnal thieves,
And how the little race of birds that hop
From fpray, to fpray, fcooping the coftlieft fruit
Infatiate, undifturb'd, Priapus' form
Avails but little ; rather guard each row
With the falfe terrors of a breathlefs kite.
This done, the timorous flock with fwifteft wing
Scud through the air ; their fancy reprefents
His mortal talons, and his rav'nous beak
Deftructive ; glad to fhun his hoftile gripe,
They quit their thefts, and unfrequent the fields.

　　Befides, the filthy fwine will oft invade
Thy firm inclofure, and with delving fnout

The rooted foreſt undermine : forthwith
Alloo thy furious maſtiff, bid him vex
The noxious herd, and print upon their ears
A ſad memorial of their paſt offence.
  The flagrant Procyon will not fail to bring
Large ſhoals of ſlow houſe-bearing ſnails, that creep
O'er the ripe fruitage, paring ſlimy tracts
In the ſleek rinds, and unpreſt Cyder drink.
No art averts this peſt ; on thee it lies
With morning and with evening hand to rid
The preying reptiles ; nor, if wiſe, wilt thou
Decline this labour, which itſelf rewards
With pleaſing gain, whilſt the warm limbic draws
Salubrious waters from the nocent brood.
  Myriads of waſps now alſo cluſtring hang,
And drain a ſpurious honey from thy groves,
Their winter food ; though oft repulſt, again
They rally undiſmay'd : but fraud with eaſe
Enſnares the noiſom ſwarms ; let ev'ry bough
Bear frequent vials, pregnant with the dregs
Of Moyle, or Mum, or Treacle's viſcous juice ;
They, by th' alluring odor drawn, in haſte
Fly to the dulcet cates, and crouding ſip
Their palatable bane ; joyful thou'lt ſee
The clammy ſurface all o'erſtrown with tribes
Of greedy inſects, that with fruitleſs toil
Flap filmy pennons oft, to extricate
Their feet, in liquid ſhackles bound, 'till death

Bereave them of their worthlefs fouls; fuch doom
Waits luxury, and lawlefs love of gain !
    Howe'ér thou may'ft forbid external force,
Inteftine evils will prevail ; damp airs,
And rainy winters, to the center pierce
Of fierceft fruits, and by unfeen decay
The proper relifh vitiate : then the grub
Oft unobferv'd invades the vital core,
Pernicious tenant ! and her fecret cave
Enlarges hourly, preying on the pulp
Ceafelefs ; mean-while the apple outward form
Delectable the witlefs fwain beguiles,
'Till, with a writhen mouth, and fpattering noife,
He taftes the bitter morfel, and rejects
Difrelifh'd ; not with lefs furprize, than when
Embattled troops with flowing banners pafs
Thro' flow'ry meads delighted, nor diftruft
The fmiling furface ; whilft the cavern'd ground,
With grain incentive ftor'd, by fudden blaze
Burfts fatal, and involves the hopes of war
In fiery whirles ; full of victorious thoughts,
Torn and difmembred, they aloft expire.
    Now turn thine eye to view Alcinous' groves,
The pride of the Phœacian ifle, from whence,
Sailing the fpaces of the boundlefs deep,
To Ariconium precious fruits arriv'd :
The Pippin burnifh'd o'er with gold, the Mofe
Of fweeteft honey'd tafte, the fair Permain,

Temper'd, like comelieft nymph, with red and
Salopian acres flourifh with a growth   (white.
Peculiar, ftyl'd the Ottley : be thou firft
This apple to tranfplant ; if to the name
It's merit anfwers, no where fhalt thou find
A wine more priz'd, or laudable of tafte.
Nor does the Eliot leaft deferve thy care,
Nor John-Apple, whofe wither'd rind, entrencht
With many a furrow, aptly reprefents
Decrepid age ; nor that from Harvey nam'd
Quick-relifhing ; why fhould we fing the Thrift,
Codling, or Pomroy, or of pimpled coat
The Ruffet, or the Cat's-Head's weighty orb,
Enormous in its growth ; for various ufe
Tho' thefe are meet, tho' after full repaft
Are oft requir'd, and crown the rich defert ?
_ What, tho' the Pear-tree rival not the worth
Of Ariconium produ
cts ? yet her freight
Is not contemn'd, yet her wide-branched arms
Beft fcreen thy manfion from the fervent dog
Averfe to life ; the wintry hurricanes
In vain imploy their roar, her trunk unmov'd
Breaks the ftrong onfet, and controls their rage.
Chiefly the Bofbury, whofe large increafe,
Annual, in fumptuous banquets claims applaufe,
Thrice acceptable bev'rage ! could but art
Subdue the floating lee, Pomona's felf   (ftrife.
Would dread thy praife, and fhun the dubious

Be it thy choice, when summer-heats annoy,
To sit beneath her leafy canopy,
Quaffing rich liquids: oh! how sweet t' enjoy,
At once her fruits, and hospitable shade!
But how with equal numbers shall we match
The Musk's surpassing worth! that earliest gives
Sure hopes of racy wine, and in its youth,
Its tender nonage, loads the spreading boughs
With large and juicy offspring, that defies
The vernal nippings, and cold syderal blasts!
Yet let her to the Red-streak yield, that once
Was of the Sylvan kind, unciviliz'd,
Of no regard, 'till Scudamore's skilful hand
Improv'd her, and by courtly discipline
Taught her the savage nature to forget:
Hence styl'd the Scudamorean plant; whose wine
Who-ever tastes, let him with grateful heart
Respect that ancient royal house, and wish
The nobler peer, that now transcends our hopes
In early worth, his country's justest pride,
Uninterrupted joy, and health entire.
Let every tree in every garden own
The Red-streak as supreme; whose pulpous fruit
With gold irradiate, and vermilion shines
Tempting, not fatal, as the birth of that
Primæval interdicted plant, that won
Fond Eve in hapless hour to taste, and die.

H

This, of more bounteous influence, infpires
Poetic raptures, and the lowly mufe
Kindles to lofty ftrains ; even I perceive
Her facred virtue. See ! the numbers flow
Eafiy, whilft, chear'd with her nectareous juice,
Hers, and my country's praifes, I exalt.
Hail, Herefordian plant, thou 'doft difdain
All other fields ! heaven's fweeteft bleffing, hail !
Be thou the copious matter of my fong,
And thy choice Nectar ; on which always waits
Langhter, and fport, and care beguiling wit,
And friendfhip, chief delight of human life.
What fhould we wifh for more ? or why, in queft
Of foreign vintage, infincere, and mix'd,
Traverfe th'extremeft world ? Why tempt the rage
Of the rough ocean ? when our native glebe
Imparts, from bounteous womb, annual recruits
Of wine delectable, that far furmounts
Gallic, or Latin grapes, or thofe that fee
The fetting fun near Calpe's tow'ring height.
Nor let the Rhodian, nor the Lefbian vines
Vaunt their rich muft, nor let Tokay contend
For fov'ranty ; Phanæus felf muft bow
To th' Ariconian vales : And fhall we doubt
T' improve our vegetable wealth, or let
The foil lye idle, which, with fit manure,
With largeft ufury repay, alone
Impower'd to fupply what nature afks

Frugal, or what nice appetite requires ;
The meadows here, with bat'ning ooze enrich'd,
Give fpirit to the grafs ; three cubits high
The jointed herbage fhoots, th' unfallow'd glebe
Yearly o'ercomes the granaries with ftore
Of golden wheat, the ftrength of human life.
Lo, on auxiliary poles, the Hops
Afcending fpiral, rang'd in meet array !
Lo, how the arable with barley grain
Stands thick, o'erfhadow'd, to the thirfty hind
Tranfporting profpect ! thefe, as modern ufe
Ordains, infus'd, an auburn drink compofe,
Wholefome, of deathlefs fame. Here, to the fight,
Apples of price, and plenteous fheaves of corn,
Oft interlac'd occur, and both imbibe
Fitting congenial juice ; fo rich the foil,
So much does fructuous moifture o'er abound !
Nor are the hills unamiable, whofe tops
To heaven afpire, affording profpect fweet
To human ken ; nor at their feet the vales
Defcending gently, where the lowing herd
Chews verd'rous pafture ; nor the yellow fields
Gaily, enterchang'd, with rich variety
Pleafing, as when an Emerald green enchas'd
In flamy gold, from the bright mafs acquires
A nobler hue, more delicate to fight.
Next add the Sylvan fhades, and filent groves,

(Haunt of the Druids) whence the hearth is fed
With copious feuel; whence the sturdy oak,
A prince's refuge once, th' eternal guard
Of England's throne, by sweating peasants fell'd,
Stems the vast main, and bears tremendous war
To distant nations, or with sov'ran sway
Awes the divided world to peace and love.
Why should the Chalybes, or Bilboa boast
Their harden'd iron; when our mines produce
As perfect martial ore? Can Timolus' head
Vie with our safron odours? Or the fleece
Bœtic, or finest Tarentine, compare
With Leinster's silken wool? Where shall we find
Men more undaunted, for their country's weal
More prodigal of life: In ancient days,
The Roman legions, and great Cæsar found
Our fathers no mean foes; and Cressy plains,
And Agincourt deep ting'd with blood, confess
What the Silures vigour unwithstood
Could do in rigid fight; and chiefly what
Brydges' wide-wasting hand, first garter'd knight,
Puissant author of great Chandois' stem,
High Chandois, that transmits paternal worth,
Prudence, and ancient prowess, and renown,
T' his noble offspring. O thrice happy peer!
That, blest with hoary vigour, view'st thy self
Fresh blooming in thy generous son; whose lips
Flowing with nervous eloquence exact,

Charm the wife fenate, and attention win
In deepeft councils : Ariconium pleas'd,
Him, as her chofen worthy, firft falutes.
Him on th' Iberian, on the Gallic fhore,
Him hardy Britons blefs ; his faithful hand
Conveys new courage from afar, nor more
The general's conduct, than his care avails.

    Thee alfo, glorious branch of Cecil's line,
This country claims ; with pride and joy to thee
Thy Alterennis calls : yet fhe endures
Patient thy abfence, fince thy prudent choice
Has fix'd thee in the mufe's faireft feat,
Where Aldrich reigns, and from his endlefs ftore
Of univerfal knowledge ftill fupplies
His noble care ; he generous thoughts inftils
Of true nobility, their country's love,
(Chief end of life) and forms their ductile minds
To human virtues : By his genius led,
Thou foon in every art pre-eminent
Shall grace this ifle, and rife to Burleigh's fame.

    Hail high-born peer ! and thou great nurfe of arts
And men, from whence confpicuous patriots fpring,
Hanmer, and Bromley ; thou, to whom with due
Refpect Wintonia bows, and joyful owns
Thy mitrid offspring ; be for ever blefs'd
With like examples, and to future times
Proficuous, fuch a race of men produce,

As, in the cafe of virtue firm, may fix
Her throne inviolate.   Hear, ye gods ! this vow
From one, the meaneft in her numerous train; _
Tho' meaneft, not leaft ftudious of her praife.

   Mufe ! raife thy voice to Beaufort's fportlefs fame,
To Beaufort's in a long defcent deriv'd
From royal anceftry, of kingly rights
Faithful afferters : In him cent'ring meet
Their glorious virtues, high defert from pride
Disjoin'd, unfhaken honour, and contempt
Of ftrong allurements.   O illuftrious prince !
O thou of antient faith ! Exulting, thee,
In her fair lift, this happy land inrolls.

   Who can refufe a tributary verfe
To Weymouth, firmeft friend of flighted worth.
In evil days ? whofe hofpitable gate,
Unbarr'd to all, invites a numerous train (crown'd,
Of daily guefts; whofe board, with plenty
Revives the feaft-rites old : mean while his care
Forgets not the afflicted, but content
In acts of fecret goodnefs, fhuns the praife,
That fure attends.   Permit me, bounteous lord,
To blazen what though hid will bounteous fhine ;
And with thy name to dignify my fong.

   But who is he, that on the winding ftream
Of Vaga firft drew vital breath, and now
Approv'd in Anna's fecret councils fits,
Weighing the fum of things, with wife forecaft

Sollicitous of public good ? How large
His mind, that comprehends whate'er was known
To old, or prefent times ; yet not elate,
Not confcious of its fkill ? what praife deferves
His liberal hand, that gathers but to give,
Preventing fuit ? O not unthankful mufe !
Him lowly reverence, that firft deign'd to hear
Thy pipe, and fkreen'd thee from opprobrious
    tongues ;
Acknowledge thy own Harley, and his name
Infcribe on ev'ry bark ; the wounded plants.
Will faft increafe, fafter thy juft refpect.

    Such are our heroes, by their virtues known,
Or fkill of peace, and war : of fofter mold
The female fex, with fweet attractive airs
Subdue obdurate hearts. The travellers oft,
That view their matchlefs forms with tranfient
    glance
Catch fudden love, and figh for nymphs unknown,
Smith with the magic of their eyes : nor hath
The Daedal hand of nature only pour'd
Her gifts of outward grace ; their innocence
Unfeign'd, and virtue moft engaging, free
From pride, or artifice, long joys afford
To th' honeft nuptial bed, and in the wane
Of life, rebate the miferies of age.
    And is there found a wretch, fo bafe a mind,
That woman's pow'rful beauty dares condemn,
Exacteft work of heaven ? he ill deferves
Or love, or pity ; friendlefs let him fee

Uneafy, tedious days, defpis'd forlorn,
As ftain of human race : but may the man,
That chearfully recounts the females praife,
Find equal love, and love's untainted fweets
Enjoy with honour. O, ye gods ! might I
Elect my fate, my happieft choice fhould be
A fair, and modeft virgin, that invites
With afpect chafte, forbidding loofe defire,
Tenderly fmiling, in whofe heavenly eye
Sits pureft love enthron'd : but if the ftars
Malignant, thefe my better hopes oppofe,
May I, at leaft, the facred pleafures know
Of ftricteft amity ; nor ever want
A friend, with whom I mutually may fhare
Gladnefs, and anguifh, by kind intercourfe
Of fpeech, and offices. May in my mind
Indelible a grateful fenfe remain
Of favours undeferv'd !—O thou ! from whom
Gladly both rich, and low feek aid ; moft wife
Interpreter of right, whofe gracious voice
Breathes equity, and curbs too rigid law
With mild, impartial reafon ; what returns
Of thanks are due to thy beneficence
Freely vouchfaf'd, when to the gates of death
I tended prone ? if thy indulgent care
Had not preven'd, among unbody'd fhades
I now had wander'd ; and thefe empty thoughts
Of apples perifh'd : but, up-rais'd by thee,

I tune my pipe afreſh, each night, and day,
Thy unexampled goodneſs to extol
Deſirous; but nor night, nor day ſuffice
For that great taſk; the highly honour'd name
Of Trevor muſt employ my willing thoughts
Inceſſant, dwell for ever on my tongue.

    Let me be grateful, but let far from me
Be fawning cringe, and falſe diſſembling look,
And ſervile flattery, that harbours oft
In courts, and gilded roofs. Some looſe the bands
Of antient friendſhip, cancel nature's laws
For pageantry, and taudry gugaws. Some
Renounce their ſires, oppoſe paternal right
For rule, and power; and other's realms invade,
With ſpecious ſhews of love. This traiterous
Betrays his ſov'ran. Others deſtitute (wretch
Of real zeal, to ev'ry altar bend,
By lucre ſway'd, and act the baſeſt things
To be ſtyl'd honourable : th' honeſt man,
Simple of heart, prefers inglorious want
To ill-got wealth; rather from door to door
A jocund pilgrim, though diſtreſs'd, he'll rove,
Than break his plighted faith, nor fear, nor hope
Will ſhock his ſtedfaſt ſoul; rather debarr'd
Each common privilege, cut off from hopes
Of meaneſt gain, of preſent goods deſpoil'd ;
He'll bear the marks of infamy, contemn'd,
Unpity'd ; yet his mind, of evil pure,
Supports him, and intention free from fraud.

If no retinue with obfervant eyes
Attend him, if he can't with purple ftain
Of cumbrous veftments, labour'd o'er with gold,
Dazle the croud, and fet them all agape ;
Yet clad in homely weeds, from envy's darts
Remote he lives, nor knows the nightly pangs
Of confcience, nor with fpectre's grifly forms,
Dæmons, and injur'd fouls at clofe of day
Annoy'd, fad interrupted flumbers finds.
But (as a child, whofe inexperienc'd age
Nor evil purpofe fears, nor knows,) enjoys
Nights fweet refrefhment, humid fleep, fincere.
When chanticleer, with clarion fhrill recals
The tardy day, he to his labours hies
Gladfome, intent on fomewhat that may eafe
Unhealthy mortals, and with curious fearch
Examines all the properties of herbs,
Foffils, and minerals, that th' embowell'd earth
Difplays, if by his induftry he can
Benefit human race ; or elfe his thoughts
Are exercis'd with fpeculations deep   (rules
Of good, and juft, and meet, and th' wholfome
Of temperance, and aught that may improve
The moral life ; not fedulous to rail,
Nor with envenom'd tongue to blaft the fame
Of harmlefs men, or fecfet whifpers fpread,
'Mong faithful friends, to breed diftruft, and hate.
Studious of virtue, he no life obferves
Except his own, his own employs his cares,

Large fubject ! that he labours to refine
Daily, nor of his little ftock denies
Fit alms to Lazars, merciful, and meek.
    Thus facred Virgil liv'd, from courtly vice,
And baits of pompous Rome fecure : at court
Still thoughtful of the rural honeft life,
And how t'improve his grounds, and how himfelf
Beft poet ! fit examplar for the tribe
Of Phœbus ; nor lefs fit Mæonides,
Poor eyelefs pilgrim ! and if after thefe,
If after thefe another I may name,
Thus tender Spenfer liv'd, with mean repaft
Content, deprefs'd by penury, and pine
In foreign realm : yet not debas'd his verfe
By fortune's frowns.   And had that other bard,
Oh, had but he that firft ennobled fong
With holy raptures, like his Abdiel been,
'Mong many faithlefs, ftrictly faithful found,
Unpity'd, he fhould not have wail'd his orbs,
That roll'd in vain to find the piercing ray,
And found no dawn, by dim fuffufion veil'd !
But he—However, let the mufe abftain,
Nor blaft his fame, from whom fhe learnt to fing
In much inferior ftrains, grov'ling beneath
Th' Olympian hill, or plains, and vales intent,
Mean follower.   There let her reft a-while,
Pleas'd with the fragrant walks, and cool retreat.

C Y D E R.

B O O K II.

O HARCOURT ! whom th' ingenuous love of
Has carry'd from thy native foil beyond (arts
T' eternal Alpine fnows, and now detains
In Italy's wafte realms, how long muft we
Lament thy abfence ? Whilft in fweet fojourn
Thou view'ft the reliques of old Rome ; or what,
Unrival'd authors by their prefence, made
For ever venerable, rural feats,
Tibur, and Tufculum, or Virgil's urn
Green with immortal bays, which haply thou,
Refpecting his great name, doft now approach
With bended knee, and ftrow with purple flow'rs;
Unmindful of thy friends, that ill can brook
This long delay.   At length, dear youth ! return,
Of wit, and judgement ripe in blooming years,
And Britain's ifle with Latian knowledge grace.
Return, and let thy father's worth excite
Thirft of pre-eminence ; fee ! how the caufe

Of widows, and of orphans he afferts
With winning rhetorick, and well-argu'd law!
Mark well his footfteps, and, like him, deferve
Thy princes favour, and thy country's love.
Mean while (altho' the Maffic grape delights
Pregnant of racy juice, and Formian hills
Temper thy cups, yet) wilt not thou reject
Thy native liquors : lo! for thee my mill
Now grinds choice apples, and the Britifh vats
O'erflow with generous Cyder; far remote
Accept this labour, nor defpife the mufe,
That, paffing lands, and feas, on thee attends.
    Thus far of trees : the pleafing tafk remains,
To fing of wines, and autumn's bleft increafe.
Th' effects of art are fhewn, yet what avails
'Gainft heaven? Oft, notwithftanding all thy care
To help thy plants, when the fmall fruit'ry feems
Exempt from ills, an oriental blaft
Difaftrous flies, foon as the hind, fatigu'd,
Unyokes his team ; the tender freight, unfkill'd
To bear the hot difeafe, diftemper'd pines
In the year's prime, the deadly plague annoys
The wide inclofure ; think not vainly now
To treat thy neighbours with mellifluous cups,
Thus difappointed : if the former years
Exhibit no fupplies, alas! thou muft
With taftlefs water wafh thy droughty throat.
                    I

A thoufand accidents the farmer's hopes
Subvert, or check; uncertain all his toil,
'Till lufty autumn's luke-warm days, allay'd
With gentle colds, infenfibly confirm
His ripening labours; autumn, to the fruits
Earth's various lap produces, vigour gives
Equal, intenerating milky grain,
Berries, and fky-dy'd plumbs, and what in coat
Rough, or foft rin'd, or bearded hufk, or fhell;
Fat Olives, and Piftacio's fragrant nut,
And the Pine's tafteful apple : autumn paints
Aufonian hills with grapes, whilft Englifh plains
Blufh with pomaceous harvefts, breathing fweets.
O let me now, when the kind early dew
Unlocks the unbofom'd odors, walk among
The well-rang'd files of trees, whofe full-ag'd ftore
Diffufe ambrofial fteams than Myrrh, or Nard
More grateful, or perfuming flow'ry Bean!
Soft whifp'ring airs, and the lark's mattin fong
Then woo to mufing, and becalm the mind
Perplex'd with irkfome thoughts. Thrice happy
Beft portion of the various year, in which (times,
Nature rejoiceth, fmiling on her works
Lovely, to full perfection wrought! but ah,
Short are our joys, and neighb'ring griefs difturb
Our pleafant hours. Inclement winter dwells
Contiguous; forth with frofty blafts deface
The blithfome year! trees of their fhrivel'd fruits

Are widow'd, dreary ſtorms o'er all prevail.
Now, now's the time ; ere haſty ſuns forbid
To work, diſburden thou thy ſapleſs wood
Of its rich progeny ; the turgid fruit
Abounds with mellow liquor ; now exhort
Thy hinds to exerciſe the pointed ſteel
On the hard rock, and give a wheely form
To the expected grinder : Now prepare
Materials for thy mill, a ſturdy poſt
Cylindric, to ſupport the grinder's weight
Exceſſive, and a flexile ſallow' entrench'd,
Rounding, capacious of the juicy hord.
Nor muſt thou not be mindful of thy preſs
Long ere the vintage ; but with timely care
Shave the goats ſhaggy beard, left thou too late
In vain ſhould'ſt ſeek a ſtrainer, to diſpart
The huſky, terrene dregs, from purer muſt.
Be cautious next a proper ſteed to find,
Whoſe prime is paſt ; the vigorous horſe diſdains
Such ſervile labours, or, if forc'd, forgets
His paſt atchievements, and victorious palms.
Blind Bayard rather, worn with work, and years,
Shall roll th' unweildy ſtone ; with ſober pace
Hell tread the circling path, 'till dewy eve,
From early day-ſpring, pleas'd to find his age
Declining, not unuſeful to his lord.
 Some, when the preſs, by utmoſt vigour ſcrew'd,
Has drain'd the pulpous maſs, regale their ſwine

With the dry refuse; thou, more wife, fhalt ſteep
Thy huſks in water, and again employ
The pondrous engine. Water will imbibe
The ſmall remains of ſpirit, and acquire
A vinous flavour; this the peaſants blithe
Will quaff, and whiſtle, as thy tinkling team
They drive and ſing of Fuſca's radiant eye, (now
Pleas'd with the medly draught. Nor ſhalt thou
Reject the Apple-Cheeſe, tho' quite exhauſt;
Even now 'twill cheriſh, and improve the roots
Of ſickly plants; nor vigour hence convey'd
Will yield an harveſt of unuſual growth.
Such profit ſprings from huſks diſcreetly us'd!

   The tender apples, from their parents rent
By ſtormy ſhocks, muſt not neglected lye
The prey of worms: A frugal man I knew,
Rich in one barren acre, which, ſubdu'd
By endleſs culture, with ſufficient muſt
His caſks repleniſh'd yearly: he no more
Deſir'd, nor wanted; diligent to learn
The various ſeaſons, and by ſkill repel
Invading peſts, ſucceſsful in his cares,
'Till the damp Libyan wind, with tempeſts arm'd
Outrageous, bluſter'd horrible amidſt
His Cyder-groves: O'er-turn'd by furious blaſts,
The ſightly ranks fall proſtrate, and around
Their fruitage ſcatter'd, from the genial boughs
Stript immature: Yet did he not repine,

Nor curſe his ſtars ; but prudent, his fall'n heaps
Collecting, cheriſh'd with the tepid wreaths
Of tedded graſs, and the ſun's mellowing beams
Rival'd with artful heats, and thence procur'd
A coſtly liquor, by improving time
Equall'd with what the happieſt vintage bears.

But this I warn thee, and ſhall always warn,
No heterogeneous mixture uſe, as ſome
With watry turneps have debas'd their wines,
Too frugal ; nor let the crude humours dance
In heated braſs, ſteaming with fire intenſe,
Although Devonia much commends the uſe
Of ſtrength'ning Vulcan ; with their native ſtrength
Thy wines ſufficient, other aid refuſe ;
And, when th' allotted orb of time's compleat,
Are more commended than the labour'd drinks.

Nor let thy avarice tempt thee to withdraw
The prieſt's appointed ſhare ; with chearful heart
The tenth of thy increaſe beſtow, and own
Heaven's bounteous goodneſs, that will ſure repay
Thy grateful duty : This neglected, fear
Signal avengeance, ſuch as over-took
A miſer, that unjuſtly once with-held
The clergy's due ; relying on himſelf,
His fields he tended with ſuccefsleſs care,
Early, and late, when, or unwiſh'd for rain
Deſcended, or unſeaſonable froſts

I 3

Curb'd his increasing hopes, or when around
The clouds dropt fatness, in the middle sky
The dew suspended staid, and left unmoist
His execrable glebe : recording this,
Be just, and wise and tremble to transgress.

　　Learn, now the promise of the coming year
To know, that by no flattering signs abus'd,
Thou wisely may'st provide : The various moon
Prophetic, and attendant stars explain
Each rising dawn ; ere icy crusts surmount
The current stream, the heavenly orbs serene
Twinkle with trembling rays, and Cynthia glows
With light unsully'd : Now the fowler warn'd
by these good omens, with swift early steps(glades
Treads the crimp earth, ranging thro' fields and
Offensive to the birds, sulphureous death　(strain
Checks their mid flight, and heedless while they
Their tuneful throats, the tow'ring, heavy lead,
O'er-takes their speed ; they leave their little lives
Above the clouds, precipitant to earth.

　　The woodcocks early visit, and abode
Of long continuance in our temperate clime,
Foretell a liberal harvest ; he of times
Intelligent, th' harsh Hyperborean ice
Shuns for our equal winters ; when our suns
Cleave the chill'd soil, he backward wings his way
To Scandinavian frozen summers, meet
For his num'd blood.　But nothing profits more

Than frequent fnows: O, may'ft thou often fee
Thy furrows whiten'd by the wooly rain
Nutricious! Secret nitre lurks within
The porous wet, quick'ning the languid glebe.

 Sometimes thou fhalt with fervent vows implore
A moderate wind; the orchat loves to wave
With winter winds, before the gems exert
Their feeble heads; the loofen'd roots then drink
Large increment, earneft of happy years.

 Now will it nothing profit to obferve
The monthly ftars, their pow'rful influence
O'er planted fields, what vegetables reign
Upon each fign. On our account has Jove
Indulgent, to all moons fome fucculent plant
Allotted, that poor, helplefs man might flack
His prefent thirft, and matter find for toil.
Now will the Corinths, now the Rafps fupply
Delicious draughts; the Quinces now, or Plums,
Or Cherries, or the fair Thifbeian fruit
Are preft to wines; the Britons fqueeze the works
Of fedulous bees, and mixing od'rous herbs
Prepare balfamic cups, to wheezing lungs
Medicinal, and fhort breath'd, antient fires.

 But, if thou'rt indefatigably bent
To toil, and omnifarious drinks would'ft brew;
Befides the orchat, every hedge, and bufh,
Affords affiftance; even afflictive Birch
Curs'd by unletter'd, idle youth, diftills

A limpid current from her wounded bark,
Profufe of nurfing fap. When folar beams
Parch thirfty human veins, the damafkt meads,
Unforc'd, difplay ten thoufand painted flowers
Ufeful in potables. Thy little fons
Permit to range the paftures ; gladly they
Will mow the Cowflip-pofies, faintly fweet,
From whence thou artificial wines fhalt drain
Of icy tafte, that, in mid fervors, beft
Slack craving thirft, and mitigate the day.

Happy Ierne ! whofe moft wholefome air
Poifons envenom'd fpiders, and forbids
The baleful toad, and viper from her fhore !
More happy in her balmy draughts, (enrich'd
With mifcellaneous fpices, and the root
For thirft abating fweetnefs prais'd,) which wide
Extend her fame, and to each drooping heart
Prefent redrefs, and lively health convey.

See, how the Belgæ, fedulous, and ftout,
With bowls of fat'ning Mum, or blifsful cups
Of kernel relifh'd fluids, the fair ftar
Of early Phofphorus falute, at noon
Jocund with frequent rifing fumes ! by ufe
Inftructed, thus to quell their native flegm
Prevailing, and engender wayward mirth.

What need to treat of diftant climes, remov'd
Far from the floping journey of the year,
Beyond Petfora, and Iflandic coafts,

Where ever during snows, perpetual shades
Of darkness, would congeal their livid blood,
Did not the Arctic tract, spontaneous yield
A cheering purple berry, big with wine,
Intensely fervent, which each hour they crave,
Spread round a flaming pile of pines, and oft
They interlard their native drinks with choice
Of strongest Brandy, yet scarce with these aids
Enabled to prevent the sudden rot
Of freezing nose, and quick decaying feet.

Nor less the sable borderers of Nile,
Nor who Taprobane manure, nor they,
Whom sunny Borneo bears, are stor'd with streams
Egregious, Rum, and Rice's spirit extract:
For here, expos'd to perpendicular rays,
In vain they covet shades, and Thrascias' gales,
Pining with Æquinoctial heat, unless,
The cordial glass perpetual motion keep,
Quick circuiting; nor dare they close their eyes,
Void of a bulky charger near their lips,
With which, in often-interrupted sleep,
Their frying blood compels to irrigate
Their dry furr'd tongues, else minutely to death
Obnoxious, dismal death, th' effect of drought!

More happy they, born in Columbus' world,
Carybbes, and they, whom the Cotton plant
With downy-sprouting vests arrays! Their woods
Bow with prodigious nuts, that give at once

Celeſtial food, and nectar; then, at hand
The Lemmon, uncorrupt with voyage long,
To vinous ſpirits added (heavenly drink !)
They with pneumatic engine, ceaſeleſs draw,
Intent on laughter ; a continual tide
Flows from th' exhilerating fount.   As, when
Againſt a ſecret cliff, with ſuddain ſhock
A ſhip is daſh'd, and leaking drinks the ſea,
Th' aſtoniſh'd mariners ay ply the pump,
No ſtay, nor reſt, 'till the wide breach is clos'd.
So they (but chearful) unfatigu'd, ſtill move
The draining ſucker, then alone concern'd,
When the dry bowl forbids their pleaſing work.
  But if to hording thou art bent, thy hopes
Are fruſtrate, ſhould'ſt thou think thy pipes will
With early limpid wine. The hordid ſtore, (flow
And the harſh draught, muſt twice endure the ſun's
Kind ſtrength'ning heat, twice winter's purging
  There are, that a compounded fluid drain (cold.
From different mixtures, Woodcock, Pippin, Moyle,
Rough Eliot, ſweet Permain, the blended ſtreams
(Each mutually correcting each) create
A pleaſurable medly, of what taſte
Hardly diſtinguiſh'd ; as the ſhow'ry arch,
With lifted colours gay, Or, Azure, Gules,
Delights, and puzzles the beholder's eye,
That views the watry brede, with thouſand ſhews
Of painture vary'd, yet's unſkill'd to tell
Or where one colour riſes, or one faints.

Some cyders have by art, or age, unlearn'd
Their genuine relifh, and of fundry vines
Affum'd the flavour; one fort counterfeits
The Spanifh product; this, to Gauls, has feem'd
The fparkling Nectar of Champaigne; with that,
A German oft has fwill'd his throat, and fworn
Deluded, that imperial Rhine beftow'd
The generous rummer, whilft the owner pleas'd,
Laughs inly at his guefts, thus entertain'd
With foreign vintage from his Cyder-cafk.

Soon as thy liquor from the narrow cells
Of clofs-preft hufks is freed, thou muft refrain
Thy thirfty foul; let none perfuade to broach
Thy thick, unwholfome, undigefted cades:
The hoary frofts, and northern blafts take care
Thy muddy bev'rage to ferene, and drive
Precipitant the bafer, ropy lees.

And now thy wine's tranfpicuous, purg'd from
Its earthly grofs, yet let it feed awhile   (all
On the fat refufe, left too foon disjoin'd
From fprightly, it, to fharp, or vapid change.
When to convenient vigour it attains,
Suffice it to provide a brazen tube
Inflext; felf-taught, and voluntary flies
The defecated liquor, through the vent
Afcending, then by downward tract convey'd,
Spouts into fubject veffels, lovely clear.

As when a moon-tide fun, with fummer beams,
Darts thro' a cloud, her watry fkirts are edg'd
With lucid amber, or undroffy gold :
So, and fo richly, the purg'd liquid fhines.
    Now alfo, when the colds abate, nor yet
Full Summer fhines, a dubious feafon, clofe
In glafs thy purer ftreams, and let them gain,
From due confinement, fpirit, and flavour new.
    For this intent, the fubtle chymift feeds
Perpetual flames, whofe unrefifted force.
O'er fand, and afhes, and the ftubborn flint
Prevailing, turns into a fufil fea,
That in his furnace bubbles funny-red :
From hence a glowing drop with hollow'd fteel
He takes, and by one efficacious breath
Dilates to a furprifing cube, or fphere,
Or oval, and fit receptacles forms
For every liquid, with his plaftic lungs,
To human life fubfervient ; by his means
Cyders in metal frail improve ; the Moyle,
And tafteful Pippin, in a moon's fhort year
Acquire compleat perfection : Now they fmoke
Tranfparent, fparkling in each drop, delight
Of curious palate, by fair virgins crav'd.
But harfher fluids different lengths of time
Expect : Thy flafk will flowly mitigate
The Eliot's roughnefs.   Stirom, firmeft fruit,
Embottled (long as Priameian Troy

Withstood the Greeks) endures, ere justly mild.
Soften'd by age, it youthful vigour gains,
Fallacious drink! Ye honest men beware,
Nor trust its smoothness: The third circling glass
Suffices virtue: But may hypocrites,
(That slyly speak one thing, another think,
Hateful as hell) pleas'd with the relish weak,
Drink on unwarn'd, 'till by inchanted cups
Infatuate, they their wily thoughts disclose,
And thro' intemperance grow a while sincere.

The farmer's toil is done; his cades mature
Now call for vent, his land exhaust permit .
T' indulge a-while. Now solemn rites he pays
To Bacchus, author of heart cheering mirth.
His honest friends, at thirsty hour of dusk,
Come uninvited; he with bounteous hand
Imparts his smoaking vintage, sweet reward
Of his own industry; the well-fraught bowl
Circles incessant, while the humble cell
With quavering laugh, and rural jests resounds.
Ease, and content, and undissembled love
Shine in each face; the thoughts of labour past
Encrease their joy. As, from retentive cage
When sullen Philomel escapes, her notes
She varies, and of past imprisonment
Sweetly complains; her liberty retriev'd
Cheers her sad soul, improves her pleasing song.

K

Gladfome they quaff, yet not exceed the bounds
Of healthy temp'rance, nor incroach on night,
Seafon of reft, but well bedew'd repair
Each to his home, with unfupplanted feet.
Ere heaven's emblazon'd by the rofy dawn
Domeftic cares awake them ; brifk they rife,
Refrefh'd, and lively with the joys that flow
From amicable talk, and moderate cups
Sweetly interchang'd.   The pining lover finds
Prefent redrefs, and long oblivion drinks
Of coy Lucinda.   Give the debtor wine ;
His joys are fhort, and few ; yet when he drinks
His dread retires, the flowing glaffes add
Courage, and mirth : magnificent in thought,
Imaginary riches he enjoys,
And in the goal expatiates unconfin'd.
Nor can the poet Bacchus' praife indite,
Debarr'd his grape: the mufes ftill require
Humid regalement, nor will aught avail
Imploring Phœbus, with unmoiften'd lips.
Thus to the generous bottle all incline,
By parching thirft allur'd : with vehement funs
When dufty fummer bakes the crumbling clods,
How pleafant is't, beneath the twifted arch
Of a retreating bow'r, in mid-days reign
To ply the fweet caroufe, remote from noife,
Secur'd of fev'rifh heats ! When th' aged year
Inclines, and Boreas' fpirit blufters frore,

Beware th' inclement heavens; nor let the hearth
Crackle with juicelefs boughs; thy ling'ring blood
Nor inftigate with th' apple's powerful ftreams.
Perpetual fhowers, and ftormy gufts confine
The willing plowman, and December warns
To annual jollities; now fportive youth
Coral incondite rhythms, with fuiting notes,
And quaver unharmonious; fturdy fwains
In clean array, for ruftic dance prepare,
Mix'd with the buxom damfels; hand in hand
They frifk, and bound, and various mazes weave,
Shaking their brawny limbs, with uncouth mein
Tranfported, and fometimes, an oblique leer
Dart on their loves, fometimes an hafty kifs
Steal from unwary laffes; they with fcorn,
And neck reclin'd, refent the ravifh'd blefs.
Mean-while, blind Britifh bards with volant touch
Traverfe loquacious ftrings, whofe folemn notes
Provoke to harmlefs revels; thefe among,
A fubtle artift ftands, in wond'rous bag
That bears imprifon'd winds, (of gentler fort
Than thofe, which erft Laertes's fon enclos'd.)
Peaceful they fleep, but let the tuneful fqueeze
Of labouring elbow roufe them, out they fly
Melodious, and with fpritely accents charm.
'Midft thefe difports, forget they not to drench
Themfelves with bellying goblets, nor when fpring

Returns, can they refuse to usher in
The fresh-born year with loud acclaim, and store
Of jovial draughts, now, when the sappy boughs
Attire themselves with blooms, sweet rudiments
Of future harvest; when the Gnossian crown
Leads on expected autumn, and the trees
Discharge their mellow burdens, let them thank
Boon nature, that thus annually supplies
Their vault, and with her former liquid gifts
Exhilerate their languid minds, within
The golden mean confin'd : beyond, there's naught
Of health, or pleasure. Therefore, when thy
Dilates, with fervent joys, and eager soul (heart
Prompts to pursue the sparkling glass, be sure
'Tis time to shun it ; if thou wilt prolong
Dire compotation ; forthwith reason quits
Her empire to confusion, and misrule,
And vain debates ; then twenty tongues at once
Conspire in senseless jargon, naught is heard
But din, and various clamour, and mad rant :
Distrust and jealousy to these succeed,
And anger-kindling taunt, the certain bane
Of well-knit friendship. Now horrid frays
Commence, the brimming glasses now are hurl'd
With dire intent ; bottles with bottles clash
In rude encounter, round their temples fly (cheeks
The sharp-edg'd fragments, down their batter'd
Mix'd Gore, and Cyder flow : what shall we say

Of rafh Elpenor, who in evil hour
Dry'd an immeafurable bowl, and thought
T' exhale his furfeit by irriguous fleep,
Imprudent? Him, death's iron-fleep opprefs'd
Defcending carelefs from his coach; the fall
Luxt his neck-joint, and fpinal marrow bruis'd.
Nor need we tell what anxious cares attend
The turbulent mirth of wine; nor all the kinds
Of maladies, that lead to death's grim cave,
Wrought by intemperance, joint-racking gout,
Inteftine ftone, and pining atrophy,
Chill, even when the fun with July-heats
Frys the fcorch'd fail, and dropfy all afloat,
Yet craving liquids: nor the Centaur's tale
Be here repeated; how with luft, and wine (fouls
Inflam'd, they fought, and fpilt their drunken
At feafting hour. Ye heav'nly pow'rs! that guard
The Britifh ifle, fuch dire events remove
Far from fair Albion, nor let civil broils
Ferment from focial cups: may we, remote
From the hoarfe, brazen found of war, enjoy
Our humid products, and with feemly draughts
Enkindle mirth, and hofpitable love.
Too oft, alas! has mutual hatred drench'd
Our fword in native blood, too oft has pride,
And hellifh difcord, and infatiate thirft
Of others rights, our quiet difcompos'd.

K 3

Have we forgot, how fell destruction rag'd
Wide-spreading, when by Eris' torch incens'd
Our fathers warr'd ? What heroes signaliz'd
For royalty, and prowess, met their fate
Untimely, undeserv'd ! How Bertie fell,
Compton, and Granvill, dauntless sons of Mars,
Fit themes of endless grief, but that we view
Their virtues yet surviving in their race !
Can we forget, how the mad, headstrong rout
Defy'd their prince to arms, nor made account
Of faith, or duty, or allegiance sworn ?
Apostate, atheist rebels ! bent to ill,
With seeming sanctity, and cover'd fraud,
Instill'd by him, who first presum'd t' oppose
Omnipotence ; alike their crime, th' event
Was not alike ; these triumph'd, and in height
Of barbarous malice, and insulting pride,
Abstain'd not from imperial blood.   O fact
Unparallel'd ! O Charles ! O best of kings !
What stars their black, disastrous influence shed
On thy nativity, that thou should'st fall
Thus, by inglorious hands, in this thy realm
Supreme and innocent, adjudg'd to death
By those, thy mercy only would have sav'd ;
Yet was the Cyder-land unstain'd with guilt ;
The Cyder-land, obsequious still to thrones,
Abhorr'd such base, disloyal deeds, and all
Her pruning-hooks extended into swords,

Undaunted, to affert the trampled rights
Of monarchy ; but, ah ! fuccefslefs fhe,
However faithful ! then was no regard
Of right, or wrong. And this once happy land,
By home bred fury rent, long groan'd beneath
Tyrannic fway, 'till fair revolving years
Our exil'd kings, and liberty reftor'd.
Now we exult, by mighty Anna's care
Secure at home, while fhe to foreign realms
Sends forth her dreadful legions, and reftrains
The rage of kings : Here, nobly fhe fupports
Juftice opprefs'd ; here, her victorious arms
Quell the ambitious : from her hand alone
All Europe fears revenge, or hopes redrefs.
Rejoice, O Albion ! fever'd from the world
By nature's wife indulgence, indigent
Of nothing from without ; in one fupreme
Intirely bleft ; and from beginning time
Defign'd thus happy ; but the fond defire
Of rule, and grandeur, multiply'd a race
Of kings, and numerous fceptres introduc'd,
Deftructive of the public weal : For now
Each potentate, as wary fear, or ftrength,
Or emulation urg'd, his neighbour's bounds
Invades, and ampler, territory feeks
With ruinous affault : on every plain
Hoft cop'd with hoft, dire was the din of war,
And ceafelefs, or fhort truce haply procur'd

By havoc, and difmay, 'till jealoufy
Rais'd new combuftion : Thus was peace in vain
Sought for by martial deeds, and conflict ftern :.
'Till Edgar grateful (as to thofe who pine
A difmal half year night, the orient beam
Of Phœbus' lamp) arofe, and into one
Cemented all the long contending powers.
Pacific monarch ; then her lovely head
Concord rear'd high, and all around diffus'd
The fpirit of love ; at eafe, the bards new ftrung
Their filent harps, and taught the woods, and
In uncouth rhythms, to echo Edgar's name. (vales,
Then gladnefs fmil'd in every eye : the years
Ran fmoothly on, productive of a line
Of wife, heroic kings, that by juft laws
Eftablifh'd happinefs at home, or crufh'd
Infulting enemies in fartheft climes.

See lyon-hearted Richard, with his force
Drawn from the north, to Jury's hallow'n plains!
Pioufly valiant, (like a torrent fwell'd
With wantry tempefts, that difdains all mounds,
Breaking a way impetuous, and involves
Within its fweep trees, houfes, men) he prefs'd
Amidft the thickeft battle ; and o'erthrew
Whate'er withftood his zealous rage ; no paufe,
No ftay of flaughter, found his vigorous arm,
But th' unbelieving fquadrons turn'd to flight
Smote in the rear, and with difhoneft wounds

Mangled behind : the Soldan, as he fled,
Oft call'd on Alla, gnaffing with defpite,
And fhame, and murmur'd many an empty curfe.

    Behold third Edward's ftreamers blazing high
On Gallia's hoftile ground ! his right with-held,
Awakens vengeance ; O imprudent Gauls !
Relying on falfe hopes, thus to incenfe
The warlike Englifh ! one important day
Shall teach you meaner thoughts : Eager of fight,
Fierce Brutus' offspring to the adverfe front
Advance refiftlefs, and their deep array
With furious inroad pierce ; the mighty force
Of Edward, twice o'erturn'd their defperate king.
Twice he arofe, and join'd the horrid fhock :
The third time, with his wide extended wings,
He fugitive declin'd fuperior ftrength,
Difcomfited ; purfu'd, in the fad chace
Ten thoufands ignominious fall ; with blood
The vallies float : great Edward thus aveng'd,
With golden Iris his broad fhield embofs'd.

    Thrice glorious prince ! whom fame with all her tongues
For ever fhall refound.   Yet from his loins
New authors of diffention fpring ; from him
Two branches, that in hofting long contend
For fov'ran fway ; (and can fuch anger dwell
In nobleft minds !) but little now avail'd
The ties of friendfhip ; every man, as led
By inclination, or vain hope, repair'd

To either camp, and breath'd immortal hate,
And dire revenge : Now horrid flaughter reigns;
Sons againft fathers tilt the fatal lance,
Carelefs of duty, and their native grounds
Diftain with kindred blood, that twanging bows
Sent fhowers of fhafts, that on their barbed points
Alternate ruin bear. Here might you fee
Barons, and peafants on th' embattled field
Slain, or half-dead, in one huge, ghaftly heap
Promifcuoufly amaft : with difmal groans,
And ejulation, in the pangs of death
Some call for aid, neglected : fome o'erturn'd
In the fierce fhock, lye gafping, and expire,
Trampled by fiery courfers ; horror thus,
And wild uproar, and defolation reign'd
Unrefpited : ah ! who at length will end
This long, pernicious fray ? What man has fate
Referv'd for this great work ? Hail, happy prince
Of Tudor's race, whom in the womb of time
Cadwallador forefaw ! Thou, thou art he,
Great Richmond Henry, that by nuptial rites
Muft clofe the gates of Janus, and remove
Deftructive difcord : now no more the drum
Provokes to arms, or trumpet's clangor fhrill
Affrights the wives, or chills the virgin's blood ;
But joy, and pleafure open to the view
Uninterrupted ! With prefaging fkill
Thou to thy own uniteft Fergus' line

By wife alliance ; from thee James defcends,
Heaven's chofen fav'rite, firft Britannic king.
To him alone, hereditary right
Gave power fupreme ; yet ftill fome feeds remain'd
Of difcontent ; two nations under one,
In laws and int'reft diverfe, ftill purfu'd
Peculiar ends, on each fide refolute
To fly conjunction ; neither fear, nor hope,
Nor the fweet profpect of a mutual gain,
Could aught avail, 'till prudent Anna faid
Let there be UNION ; ftrait with reverence due
To her command they willingly unite,
One in affection, laws and government,
Indiffolubly firm ; From Dubris fouth,
To northern Orcades, her long domain.

And now thus leagu'd by an eternal bond,
What fhall retard the Britons bold defigns,
Or who fuftain their force ; in union knit,
Sufficient to withftand the powers combin'd
Of all this globe ! At this important act
The Mauritanian and Cathaian kings
Already tremble, and th' unbaptiz'd Turk
Dreads war from utmoft Thule ; uncontroul'd
The Britifh navy thro' the ocean vaft
Shall wave her double crofs, t' extremeft climes
Terrific, and return with odorous fpoils
Of Araby well fraught, or Indus' wealth,
Pearl, and Barbaric gold : mean while the fwains

Shall unmolested reap, what plenty strows
From well stor'd horn, rich grain, and timely fruits.
The elder year, Pomona, pleas'd, shall deck
With ruby-tinctur'd births, whose liquid store
Abundant, flowing in well blended streams,
The natives shall applaud; while glad they talk
Of baleful ills, caus'd by Bellona's wrath
In other realms; where e'er the British spread
Triumphant banners, or their fame has reach'd
Diffusive, to the utmost bounds of this
Wide universe, Silurian Cyder borne
Shall please all tastes, and triumph o'er the vine.

F I N I S.

ImThe Story.com

Personalized Classic Books in many genre's

Unique gift for kids, partners, friends, colleagues

Customize:

- Character Names
- Upload your own front/back cover images (optional)
- Inscribe a personal message/dedication on the
  inside page (optional)

Customize many titles Including
- Alice in Wonderland
- Romeo and Juliet
- The Wizard of Oz
- A Christmas Carol
- Dracula
- Dr. Jekyll & Mr. Hyde
- And more...

CPSIA information can be obtained
at www.ICGtesting.com
Printed in the USA
BVHW040725121218
535350BV00015B/195/P